Social Democracy

Eunice Goes

agenda
publishing

To Inês and Philippe

First published in 2024 by Agenda Publishing
Reprinted 2024

Agenda Publishing Limited
PO Box 185
Newcastle upon Tyne
NE20 2DH
www.agendapub.com

ISBN 978-1-78821-615-9 (hardcover)
ISBN 978-1-78821-616-6 (paperback)

British Library Cataloguing-in-Publication Data
A catalogue record for this book is available from the British Library

Typeset by JS Typesetting Ltd, Porthcawl, Mid Glamorgan
Printed and bound in the UK by 4edge Ltd

Social Democracy

Short Histories

Agenda Short Histories are incisive and provocative introductions to topics, ideas and events for students wanting to know more about how we got where we are today.

Published

Conservatism
Mark Garnett

Social Democracy
Eunice Goes

Thatcherism
Peter Dorey

Contents

Acknowledgements

Writing this book would not have been possible without the support, encouragement and insights I received from family, friends, colleagues and the scholars of social democracy. First, I would like to thank my editor, Alison Howson, for taking a chance on me. She challenged me to write a short history of European social democracy and I accepted. As the process was often stressful, occasionally terrifying but ultimately rewarding, I am very grateful for her support and encouragement from the proposal stage to the final manuscript. I am also grateful for the support I received from the team at Agenda Publishing, namely from Steven Gerrard and Dan Harding.

My second big debt is to all the scholars of European social democracy from whom I learned so much over the years. I am especially grateful to Adam Przeworski, Sheri Berman, Donald Sassoon, Geoff Eley, William Smaldone, Gøsta Esping-Anderson, Stephanie Mudge, Gerasimos Moschonas, Albert S. Lindemann and Hans Keman, whose work guided me in my interpretation of the history of European social democracy. Indeed, their work helped me identify the key moments in the history of social democracy and directed me to the relevant sources that dealt with the specific country experiences of social democracy. Given the tight turnaround period to write this volume this guidance was precious. I am also grateful for everything that I learned about the different varieties of European social democracy from the experts of the specific social democratic parties. Obviously, all mistakes in this volume are my own.

I also would like to thank Ania Skrzypek, director for research and training at the Federation of European Progressive Studies, for inviting me to join the Next Left Focus Group, which has enabled me to meet scholars and experts of social democracy from many European countries and participate in many discussions about the past, present and future of social democracy. These exchanges allowed me to learn a great deal about the different experiences of social democracy. I am particularly grateful to Brian Shaev for his explanation of the German SPD's competition policy, to Dimitris Tsarouhas for guiding me through Sweden's Rehn–Meidner model and to Marius Ostrowski for the illuminating conversations on the contribution of Eduard Bernstein to social democracy. I am also grateful for the suggestions made by the anonymous reviewers of the volume at both the proposal and finalization stages of this volume.

I owe a big thanks to Maria João Rodrigues, Patrick Diamond, Rob Manwaring, Luke Martell, Karl Pike, Nick Garland, Feliz Butzlaff, Anna Paczeniask, Marco Lisi, David Klemperer, Mark Wickham-Jones, Magnus Feldman, Jonas Hinnfors, Cristina Leston-Bandeira, Jelena Pivovarova and Madalene Resende-Meyer for all that I have learned during our conversations and for their encouragement and support.

Writing this book would have not been possible without the friendship, patience and support of Michèle Cohen, Maaike Veen, Helen Redesdale and Dionyssis Dimitrakopoulos. Last but not least, I am forever grateful for the loving support and encouragement of my partner Philippe Marlière and my daughter Inês, who in the last 20 years has given me daily reasons to believe that a better world is possible.

Abbreviations

EC   European Communities
EP   European Parliament
EU   European Union
GDP   gross domestic product
MSzP Magyarországi Szociáldemokrata Párt (Hungary's Social Democratic Party)
PASOK Panhellenic Socialist Movement (Greece)
PCF   Parti Communiste Français (French Communist Party)
PCI   Partito Comunista Italianno (Italian Communist Party)
PDS   Partito Democratico di Sinistra (Italian Democratic Party of the Left)
PES   Party of European Socialists
PS   Partido Socialista (Portugal's Socialist Party)
PSF   Parti Socialist Français (French Socialist Party)
PSI   Partito Socialista Italianno (Italian Socialist Party)
PSOE Partido Socialista Obrero Español (Spain's Socialist and Workers' Party)
PvdA Partij van de Arbeid (Dutch Labour Party)
SAP   Sveriges Socialdemokratiska Arbetareparti (Sweden's Social Democratic Party)
SDP   Suomen Sosialidemokraattinen Puolue (Finland's Social Democratic Party)
SFIO Section Française de L'Ouvrière International (French Section of the Workers' International
SLD   Sojusz Lewicy Demokratyczne (Poland's Democratic Left Alliance)
SPD   Sozialdemokratische Partei Deutschlands (Germany's Social Democratic Party)

SPÖ   Sozialdemokratische Partei Österreichs (Austrian Social Democratic Party)

UBI   universal basic income

USPD   Unhabhängige Sozialdemokratische Partei Deutschlands (Independent Social Democratic Party of Germany)

Introduction: European social democracy – a story in four acts

Social democracy is an ideology and political movement that emerged in Europe in the mid-nineteenth century in response to the processes of industrialization and democratization, and which shaped the politics of the continent ever since (Eley 2002; Keman 2017). Indeed, social democracy is behind the drive for universal suffrage, the development of comprehensive welfare systems and a tamed form of capitalism, although, obviously, and as this volume explains, the genealogy of these developments is eclectic.

The variation in the timing of these big social, economic and political changes meant that social democracy emerged in many shapes and guises and spread at a different pace across Europe. However, it is possible to just about identify a rough point of origin. The economic, political and ideological revolution that paved the way for social democracy was led by Britain, France and Germany. As Lindemann explained, "economically the British paved the way; politically the French offered the most influential model" and both "provided the context for modern socialist ideas" (1983: 8) to spread across the continent. Finally, as Engels suggested, Germany, where the first social democratic party emerged, offered the template for the practice of social democratic politics (1978 [1895]: 565).

The rise of social democracy roughly accompanied the processes of industrialization and democratization which were quite advanced in Britain but far less so in Russia, Spain, Sweden and even France. The process of industrialization provoked great demographic changes, which led to political transformations. Broadly speaking, those demographic changes were about the large exodus of workers from rural areas into urban centres. Those workers found themselves uprooted from their families, friends and familiar places, working in extremely

1

harsh conditions in the new factories for a barely living wage but with no political voice and therefore without the power to transform their own lives.

In many ways their lives and lack of agency were not very different from the lives of European propertyless peasants, workers and paupers since immemorial times. What was different this time was that the ideals of the French Revolution, notably the principles of the Declaration of the Rights of Man and of the Citizen, as well as the liberal values that were empowering an assertive new political class, suggested that this state of affairs was not God-given and could be changed.

If this new class of workers found a motivation to fight for different life conditions, their struggle was neither easy nor straightforward. The 1815 Congress of Vienna seemed to have re-established Europe's old aristocratic order following the upheaval of the French Revolution of 1789, but by the 1830s it was clear that the "genie of revolution" could not be put back in the bottle. The moneyed middle classes wanted to participate in politics, and so did the artisans, liberal professionals, students, factory workers and pauperized seasonal workers who now lived in expanding European cities. From Paris to Athens, from Lisbon to Warsaw, a diverse coalition of activists demanded the right to participate in political decision-making, the right to debate freely the ideas that thus far had been shared in illegal pamphlets and books, and the right to aspire to a different society.

This movement for change was expressed in different ways across Europe. In Britain, the Chartists were leading the charge with their demands for universal manhood suffrage, secret ballots and shorter working days. In France, the silk-weavers of Lyon, an amalgam of republican and Jacobin radicals, organized and joined street protests in Paris and other cities to demand the right to vote and new economic rights. In Lisbon, Madrid and Barcelona, liberal professionals, artisans and even some of the soldiers and aristocrats who had fought the Napoleonic armies started to question the authority of absolutist monarchs. This popular unrest culminated in the slow but sure establishment of constitutional monarchies across Europe and in the gradual extension of the right to vote to a growing bourgeois class. In some parts of Europe – Belgium, Poland, Greece – the social unrest driven by the crisis of the old European monarchies and within the Ottoman empire led to the emergence of new independent countries.

Having helped the bourgeois class gain the right to vote and to partic-ipate in the political life of their nations, the European working classes felt excluded from the new constitutional settlements. They realized that the newly empowered bourgeois class and liberal parties were not inter-ested in promoting the interests of workers and of propertyless citizens, and least of all were they interested in their emancipation. It was from this nascent but clear political awakening of the working classes that European social democracy emerged.

Explaining social democratic change

This book tells the story of the theory and practice of European social democracy since its emergence in the mid-nineteenth century until our current times in a succinct and accessible fashion. In this volume, social democracy is presented as both an ideology and a political practice. Because political parties are, as Sheri Berman argued, the main "car-riers" of ideologies and the main vehicle through which they achieve political prominence (2006: 11), this volume focuses on social dem-ocratic parties. However, it also discusses other contributors to social democracy, namely intellectuals, activists, trade unions and any other organization that shaped European social democracy.

This brief volume does not offer original historical insights (as it relies mostly on secondary sources), nor does it seek to chart the twists and turns of all European social democratic parties and of social dem-ocratic thinking. This would be an impossible task for such a short vol-ume. Instead, this work builds on the vast and truly excellent literature on the subject[1] and proposes a succinct analytical map to understand the transformation of European social democracy over four distinct phases (or acts), each of them marked by a moment of change, from its emergence in the mid-nineteenth century to the 2020s.

This story of the transformation of social democracy is informed by historical institutionalism, which focuses on the interplay of ideas, insti-tutions and considerations about power to explain processes of change. As Hall and Taylor argued, historical institutionalists normally "locate institutions in a causal chain of events that accommodates a role for other factors, notably socioeconomic development and the diffusion of ideas" (1996: 942). Applying this insight to the analysis of ideologies means that we can explain the transformation of social democracy as a process that has been mostly driven by how political actors tried to deliver a social democratic conception of society while responding to the socioeconomic, political and cultural changes of their time and with the resources available to them.

Moreover, historical institutionalism tends to view institutional development as a path-dependent process. The emphasis on path dependence implies, as Pierson explained, "that history matters", that "specific patterns of timing and sequence matter", that "starting from similar conditions, a wide range of outcomes may be possible" and that "large consequences may result from relatively 'small' or contingent events" (Pierson 2000: 251). In the process, institutions develop specific ways of thinking and functioning. Consequently, change does not happen easily because the circumstances in which an institution (which can be a political party but also a set of ideas) emerges shape how it develops across time. As Pierson put it, "once established, basic outlooks on politics, ranging from ideologies to particular understandings of governments or orientations towards political groups or parties are generally tenacious" (2000: 260). For social democratic parties, their histories and socialist values and doctrines worked as constraints to change. This does not mean that change did not happen (it did). What it means is that when change happened the process was protracted and shaped by different interpretations of socialist doctrines and by the historical *acquis* of social democratic parties.

Drawing on Przeworski's authoritative analysis of the transformation of social democracy (1993: 22–3), the central thesis of the book is that social democracy is a variety of socialism that has metamorphosed because of the dialectical interplay between doctrinal commitments to a socialist vision of society and the implications of pursuing those goals through parliamentary democracy.

The second argument of the book follows from the first. Pursuing socialism via the parliamentary road inevitably shaped the development of social democracy in Europe. As Przeworski (1993) argued, the fact that social democratic parties were forced to build diverse coalitions of supporters meant that from the moment they were participating in elections they were transforming social democratic values and aims. In other words, democratic pressure meant that social democratic parties had to constantly adapt their doctrines, theories and practices to the political, economic, social and cultural circumstances they encountered on the ground.

This process of transformation was neatly summarized by Przeworski as "revolution, reform, and resignation" (2001), to which a fourth phase of "disorientation" can be added. In the permanent negotiation between different interpretations of doctrines and values, historical trajectories and considerations about power not only defined social democracy but can also explain why its history is marked by internal divisions, passionate doctrinal debates and permanent angst about ideological revisionism and reform.

But this explanation of change risks overemphasizing the role of contingency and/or of exogenous shocks and downplays the role of agency. In truth, like all political actors, the agents of social democracy were not at the complete mercy of events. They had agency, and their choices reflected their own priorities and aspirations, as well as their own interpretations of what constituted the most important challenge of the time and the most ideologically appropriate response to it.

More often than not, social democratic parties chose the incremental path to change. But as Streeck and Thelen have shown, transformative change can also occur following the accumulation of imperceptible, gradual but deliberate steps (2010: 18) which can reveal the agency of political actors. Indeed, displacement, drift, layering and conversion, which result from choices made by political actors, can have a transformational effect on institutions[2] (not only bricks and mortar institutions but also on ideologies and belief systems). For example, some doctrinal commitments, such as the pledge to overthrow capitalism, remained in the programmes of parties until the 1950s, but they were largely neglected in terms of practice. This process of drift was gradual and barely noticeable but eventually it resulted in a substantial revision of social democratic doctrine. Similarly, social democratic parties added new elements to the original doctrinal basis of social democracy. This layering effect, which was especially visible in social democratic parties' approach to the role of the state in the economy, resulted too in significant changes to the theory and practice of European social democracy. Social democratic parties also had to adapt to new political and economic circumstances and often this involved a process of "conversion" to the practices and values of other institutions, as happened in the 1990s when they had to respond to the neoliberal turn of the

European Union. Finally, layering, drift and conversion contributed to the transformation and occasional displacement of both social democratic ends and means.

European social democracy's different metamorphoses were mostly the result of reactions to contingent events and exogenous factors, but also of the different ways a diverse range of political actors interpreted and negotiated the pursuit of specific ideological aims with the need to gain the support of a sufficiently broad coalition of supporters that enabled social democrats to gain power. In short, both the commitment to social democratic doctrine and its pursuit through democratic means have been the main drivers of change; but each element pushes in a different direction. The process of change results then from the dialectical relation between the two.

Thus, this volume shows how the doctrine of social democracy was revised and, in some instances, reformed to respond to electoral challenges, namely to a changing electorate and to the recognition that to conquer power social democratic parties could not rely exclusively on the support of working-class voters. But because social democrats have been committed to socialist goals, each moment of revisionism and/or reform was preceded by agonizing debates about the ideological consistency of the proposed reforms. This constant dialectical process explains not only social democracy's different phases but also how each distinct phase resulted in a reform that led to a dilution of its means and ends.

In each revisionist stage, the meaning of social democracy was transformed. Over time, social democracy ceased to be an ideology and political phenomenon that sought to radically transform society to merely become committed to the general improvement of the living and working conditions of workers and citizens in general. This constant reassessment of ends and means meant that social democrats rarely challenged the status quo. The policies that became associated with social democracy went with the grain of capitalist economies and "bourgeois" democracies. In some cases, this incremental approach led to the emergence of a different type of capitalism which was compatible with socialism's emancipatory ideal, but in most cases, gradualism reflected the acceptance and the conviction that a radical transformation of society was an unlikely possibility. As a result, twentieth-first-century social democracy is very different from nineteenth-century social democracy, not only in terms of the problems and challenges it faces but also in terms of goals it tries to achieve. To render this process of change clear, this volume divides the history of social democracy in four distinct "acts", each of them embodying a distinct phase in the history of European social democracy.

Varieties of social democracy

This volume also seeks to account for the different varieties of European social democracy. Because the processes of democratization and industrialization happened at different times across Europe, social democracy developed at different speeds across the continent and produced a variety of social democracies (Esping-Andersen 1985; Keman 2017). Instead of a "single" model of social democracy, this volume identifies and discusses five main varieties of social democratic parties. Each one of them reflects the circumstances and the political cultures in which they emerged.

Social democratic parties were particularly strong in the industrialized countries of northern and central Europe but weaker in southern Europe where industrialization and the spread of mass education lagged northern Europe (Smaldone 2020: 103; Eley 2002: 64, Lipset 1983). Similarly, democratization is seen as a prerequisite for social democracy (Keman 2017: 29). However, the correlation between industrialization/ democratization and social democratic growth is not always straightforward. In other words, social democracy did not always spread and implanted itself faster in the countries with the most industrialized economies and most solid liberal constitutions. In fact, Donald Sassoon claims that there is a negative statistical correlation between the two variables (1997: 9). For instance, in the weakly industrialized Italy, the Socialist Party, established in 1892, had conquered one-fifth of the electorate by 1904, while Britain, with a more advanced industrialized economy and a stronger trade union movement, had no significant socialist party until 1900 (Sassoon 1997: 9). Similarly, social democratic parties were very successful in Ukraine, Finland and Norway, which were countries with sizeable peasantries and small industries. These examples show that the determining factors in the development of social democracy in Europe were political (Sassoon 1997: 9) and constitutional (i.e., the existence of parliamentary institutions, male suffrage, etc.) (Eley 2002: 64; Marks *et al.* 2009).

The variables that determined the unevenness in the spread of social democratic parties across Europe also resulted in different varieties of social democracy. In particular, the type of social democratic party that emerged was a by-product of democratization and political liberalization, of the nature of the social class system before industrialization (Lipset 1983), of the strength of socialist links to trade unions (Marks *et al.* 2009) and of the sequence in which these developments occurred (Bartolini 2007: 397). According to Lipset, "where the working class was denied full political and economic citizenship, strong revolutionary movements developed"; conversely, "the more readily working-class organizations were accepted into the economic and political order, the less radical their initial and subsequent ideologies" (Lipset 1983: 2). This was so because social democratic parties with institutional links to strong unions tended to follow a reformist path, because unions operated within the capitalist system of wage labour and were responsive to the "legal climate" (Marks *et al.* 2009: 619). On the other hand, when unions were repressed, "socialist parties led unions to revolutionism, or unions assumed the task themselves by turning to revolutionary syndicalism" (Marks *et al.* 2009: 620; see also Bartolini 2007). Similarly, Bartolini argued that "political repression was one of the main determinants of the early socialist movement behaviours and the instrument through which the state shaped the structure and fundamental forms of labour protest" (2007: 397). The type of social democratic party that emerged in Britain, Sweden and Italy or Spain seems to confirm Lipset's and Bartolini's arguments.

To a large extent this typology of social democracy remains in place. Germany's Marxist-inspired Social Democratic Party (SPD) was hugely influential in Austria, Belgium and to a smaller extent (and only during the interwar period) in the new countries that emerged following the collapse of the Austro-Hungarian Empire in 1918, namely Hungary and Czechoslovakia. This type of social democracy was supported by a large, strong and subordinate trade union movement that was formally committed to Marxism until the 1950s, although it had practised a revisionist form of social democracy since the 1920s.

The Scandinavian social democratic parties were also quite unique in their interpretation of socialism. Very quickly they abandoned the Marxism of their earlier days, which they had "copied" from the German SPD and adopted "catch-all" electoral strategies that sought to address the fact that the industrial working class did not constitute a majority in their societies. Nonetheless, Scandinavian social democracy was shaped by the strong cooperation between the organized labour movement and the social democratic party (Keman 2017: 35). Coming to terms with this reality meant that these parties implemented social democratic programmes that sought to reform capitalism and achieve equality through democratic means (Bergström 1992: 133; Molin 1992: xx).

The British Labour tradition on the other hand, which influenced similar parties in Ireland and the Netherlands as well as in Australia and New Zealand, owed more to social liberalism, Fabianism and the reformism of trade unions than to Marxism. Thus "labourism" was an ideology-light variety of social democracy which rejected the concepts of class struggle and revolution and pursued reformist strategies. As Keman explained, reformism entailed the pursuit of societal change to be "brought about within the existing 'rules of the game'" (2017: 9).

In France and in the countries of southern Europe, social democratic parties were equally ideologically eclectic, but the influences were more radical. To start with, in southern Europe social democratic parties developed independently from the trade unions (Keman 2017: 36), which in turn led to the emergence of a more radical form of social democracy. Alongside the French interpretation of Marxism, social democracy in southern Europe was influenced by republicanism, syndicalism and anarchism. These influences led to a more confrontational approach to the management of industrial relations and to an emphasis on republican and secular values.

In the 1990s, a new variety of social democratic party emerged in the former communist countries of the Baltic and central and eastern Europe which was quite distinct from other variants. As parties that were formed following the collapse of communist regimes, they were quick to dissociate themselves from any vestiges of Marxism and communism and had tenuous links to trade unions. This was particularly true for those social democratic parties that evolved out of the shell of the former communist parties that had been in power during the communist era. As such, these parties were keen to demonstrate that they were committed to democracy and to market economies. In programmatic terms this meant that the social democratic parties of former communist countries supported neoliberal policies in the shape of programmes of privatization, economic liberalization and the retrenchment of the welfare state (Tavits & Letki 2009), and some adopted authoritarian approaches to social issues such as gender equality, minority rights and civil liberties (Vachudova 2013; Holmes & Lightfoot 2011).

A question of semantics

As an ideology and political movement which was literally being formed in the streets, coffee-houses and assembly rooms of Paris, London, Berlin, Madrid, Frankfurt and Vienna in the mid-nineteenth century, social democracy was difficult to pin down. A variety of social-ist, anarchist, liberal and republican traditions were driven by the same frustrations and inspired by similar ideals of workers' emancipation but disagreed about the road map to that better world. In the end, as Przeworski argued, the main difference between social democrats and other socialist and radical traditions was their approach to political institutions (1993: 7–8).

Unlike anarchists and utopian socialists, social democrats argued that socialist ends could only be achieved through an active and relent-less pursuit of political power, which in turn led to the development of political parties which would participate in elections and gain rep-resentation in national parliaments. Unlike communists, they pursued socialist goals through the ballot box and the direct involvement in the institutions of the state, but unlike republicans and social liberals, they were committed to collective ownership of the means of production and the overthrow of capitalism. By the mid-nineteenth century, social democracy was also associated with the extension of democracy. Thus, social democracy was not only about the pursuit of socialism through democracy; it also sought to socialize democracy (Eley 2002: 22).

At this stage, it is possible to identify the main distinctive traits of social democracy. However, establishing its exact contours remains a difficult task because its policies and ideology kept evolving across time. The term "social democracy" appeared in France in the after-math of the 1848 revolution, but it only gained wider currency follow-ing the foundation of Germany's SPD in 1875[3] and the launch of the Second International in 1889. Thus, if in the 1840s social democracy was pejoratively seen as a manifestation of "bourgeois" politics, by the 1870s it was perceived as a radical ideology which argued that the class struggle, the abolition of private property, the overthrow of capitalism and the emancipation of the working classes could be achieved through the democratic conquest of political power. By 1918, social democrats rejected violent revolutionary means and were fully committed to the parliamentary road to socialism; by the 1950s social democrats accepted that socialist ideals could be delivered through a form of regulated capitalism which encompassed a mixed economy and a welfare state, but since the end of the twentieth century they have been vaguely committed to socialist values which were supposed to be delivered within the constraints of globalized capitalism and liberal democracy.

Social democracy also came to be associated with a set of values or a morphology; that is, the way a set of core, adjacent and peripheral values are "bunched together" to propose a conception of the good life (Freeden 1998). It is the way those concepts or values are "bunched together" that gives meaning and definition to ideologies. The concept of morphology allows for change, namely the introduction of new interpretations of those values as well as their reordering. However, if core concepts are abandoned, the structure of the ideology "may snap" (Freeden 1998).

In its first iteration, socialism was an ideology that sought the emancipation of the workers of the world in a society defined by equality, cooperation and fellowship. As capitalism was the greatest obstacle to that emancipation, socialists defended the organization of society around cooperation and common ownership of the means of production, which required the overthrow of capitalism. With time, other values were associated with socialism: the abolition of class differences, the promotion of democracy and equality.

This constellation of values was not valued equally by all. For example, Marx and Engels questioned the commitment to equality. In their view, this notion of equality was a less ambitious objective than the commitment to abolish class differences. In his "Critique of the Gotha Programme", Marx decried the language of equal rights as "beset with bourgeois limitations". As he explained, the language of equal rights amounts to "a right to inequality", because it is a right that "acknowledges no distinctions of class" and "tacitly recognizes unequal individual talent" (Marx 1996: 214). Similarly, Engels dismissed the egalitarianism of the SPD as a "superficial French idea" (Engels 1934 [1875]: 337). As he put it in a letter to Bebel, this was "an idea which was justified as a stage of development in its own time and place but which, like all superficial ideas of the earlier socialist schools, should now be overcome" (Engels 1934 [1875]: 337). On the other hand, he argued there would always "exist a certain inequality in the conditions of life which can be reduced to a minimum but never entirely removed" (Engels 1934 [1875]: 336).

The reasoning of Marx and Engels was duly ignored by the European social democratic parties. The language of equality was deployed in most political programmes, was widely used in speeches and pamphlets written by European social democrats and became the cardinal value of European social democracy. With time too, the commitment to emancipation disappeared from the social democratic lexicon, only making rare appearances in speeches and party programmes.

Interestingly, the term social democrat still provokes ambivalent reactions. It has been embraced by some political parties and is applied by the scholars of social democracy to mean the pursuit of socialist goals through democracy within the confines of a regulated capitalist economy. However, it is still deployed as a term of abuse by some activists, both within and outside social democratic parties. In some national contexts (e.g., in Britain and France), social democrats are portrayed as moderates and not fully committed socialists.

The story of European social democracy in four acts

The story of social democracy in four acts proposed in this volume is presented in the following sequence. Chapter 1 charts the first act of European social democracy. It starts by analysing the political context that led to the emergence of a social democratic movement in the second half of the nineteenth century and proceeds to explain how social democratic parties adapted to parliamentary democracy. In the process, the chapter argues that the impact of the First World War and of the Bolshevik Revolution led to the first big revision of the theory and practice of social democracy.

Chapter 2 examines the second act of the history of social democracy, tellingly defined by another doctrinal schism. This schism had the effect of officially establishing social democracy as a reformist and revisionist ideology which no longer aimed to overthrow capitalism and abolish private property. However, social democracy still retained a critical attitude to capitalism and became associated with the development of the welfare state, economic democracy, the mixed economy and egalitarian policies, which amounted to a very different type of capitalism from the one earlier socialist theorists had experienced, studied and conspired against. This chapter charts the debates, events and policies that set in motion this doctrinal revisionism and assesses the electoral performance and programmatic dilemmas of European social democratic parties in this period. The chapter concludes by examining the factors that led to the demise of the revisionist social democracy in the late 1970s and early 1980s.

Chapter 3 examines the third act of the history of social democracy which started in the 1980s. This phase involved the uncritical embrace of free market capitalism and the move away from egalitarian goals both in terms of political practice and doctrine. The chapter examines the factors that drove this move, namely the fall of the Berlin Wall, the triumph of neoliberalism, the impact of globalization, the process of European integration and the changes to the electoral coalitions of social democratic parties which led to a reassessment of electoral strategies. The chapter also analyses the intellectual debates surrounding the "Third Way" as well as the emergence of a new variety of social democratic party in the post-communist countries of the Baltic and eastern and central Europe. Finally, the chapter assesses the impact of these factors on social democratic theory and practice.

Chapter 4 analyses the causes of the crisis that engulfed European social democracy since the global financial crisis of 2008. Since then, Europe has experienced more than a decade of multiple crises which have been detrimental to the electoral success of social democratic parties, but which paradoxically have also opened the possibility for social democratic ideological renewal. The combination of multiple crises and the ideological disorientation means that the fourth act of European social democracy is still being written.

The Conclusion charts the ideological evolution of social democracy since its origins until current times and explains the factors that drove that transformation. This chapter analyses the political, economic and electoral challenges that social democracy currently faces and suggests that social democratic parties have a range of options that may result either in the end of social democracy or in its renewal.

1

Socialism via the parliamentary road

Social democracy only entered the European political lexicon in the 1870s, but there were earlier references to the term. Following the 1848 revolution, which established France's Second Republic, the word social democrat referred to the coalition between the republicans of the Mountain (La Montagne) and democratic socialists (Moschonas 2002: 17). However, its usage was rather limited across Europe. Far more common was the term socialism, of which several varieties existed.

More importantly, the term social democracy was used in a derogatory fashion by communists and revolutionary socialists. For example, in "The Eighteenth Brumaire of Louis Bonaparte", Karl Marx explained that democratic socialists known as the La Montagne had drafted a programme that had removed "the revolutionary sting" from "the social demands of the proletariat" (Marx 1996 [1852]: 38). The implication of this was that social democracy was merely about "the reform of society in a democratic way, but a reform within petty-bourgeois limits" (Marx 1996 [1852]: 59). In short, social democracy was a bourgeois project. But as Friedrich Engels admitted in 1894, "things are different, and this word may perhaps do the job even though it remains inexact" (Engels quoted by Lenin 1992 [1917]: 7). Leaving aside Engels's concerns about its exact semantic value, what is clear is that by the 1870s social democracy not only came to mean something very different from its earlier reformist connotations but it also gained wider currency within European radical political circles.

This chapter charts the emergence of social democracy as a political movement and ideology in Europe from the 1870s. It starts by briefly explaining the political, social and ideational context in which it emerged. Next, it maps its beginnings from the foundation of the first social democratic party – Germany's Social Democratic Workers' Party – to the spread of social democratic parties across Europe. The chapter also examines how social democrats navigated the doctrinal tensions created by their entry into electoral politics. Debates about conquering political power through the ballot box, the prospect of revolution or the promises of reform, and the potential cooperation with liberal parties gradually transformed social democracy. Finally, the chapter explains the impact of rising nationalism in Europe, the First World War and the Bolshevik Revolution on social democracy.

Along the way, the chapter shows that social democracy did not evolve in a neat and linear form in the European continent. Because democratization and industrialization happened at different times and in different ways across Europe, the evolution and growth of social democracy as a political force was not a uniform phenomenon.

Setting the stage

Like all ideologies, social democracy emerged and evolved in response to specific political, economic, social and cultural circumstances. As an ideology and political movement that represented the interests of workers, social democracy was inspired by the ideals of the French Revolution and Enlightenment and was shaped by the impact of the Industrial Revolution and the spread of representative democracy, which in turn transformed European societies (Hobsbawm 1995a: 2).

The nineteenth century was a period of great hope for the European left. The words of socialist and anarchist thinkers as varied as Charles Fourier, Robert Owen, Henri de Saint-Simon, Louis Blanc, Pierre-Joseph Proudhon, William Morris, Ferdinand Lassalle and Mikhail Bakunin inspired and mobilized trade unionists, workers and political activists all over Europe. But if the words of radical thinkers were inspiring, the campaigns for universal male suffrage and a shorter working week, led by the Chartist movement in Britain, showed that improving workers' lives was a realistic prospect. Uniting this eclectic bunch of activists and thinkers was the common belief that the best way to achieve workers' emancipation was by organizing society as a cooperative endeavour where all would be given the chance to flourish.

During what McLellan aptly called the "springtime of socialist thought" (1998: xvi), Karl Marx and Friedrich Engels set up the Communist Correspondence Committee, which provided a discussion forum for a group of German, British and French socialists, artisans and trade unionists. When the correspondence committee became the Communist League in 1847, Marx was given the task of writing a programme, which he hastily co-drafted with Engels and published in February of 1848. That programme, which became a call to arms, was *The Communist Manifesto.*

In this text, Marx and Engels argued that the proletarian classes had reached the moment in their evolution where they were ready for the revolution which would overthrow the capitalist order and set the stage for workers' emancipation. As they put it, "in depicting the most general phases of development of the proletariat, we traced the more or less veiled civil war, raging within the existing society, up to the point where the war breaks out into open revolution, and where the violent overthrow of the bourgeoisie lays the foundation for the sway of the proletariat" (Marx & Engels 1998 [1848]: 15). In their view, that revolutionary moment was near. Crucially, they insisted that the revolutionary path to communism led by the proletariat was the key difference between communists and "utopian socialists" (Engels 1969 [1880]: 112). This key difference reflected a distinct understanding of historical evolution. Marx and Engels's materialist conception of history assumed that the transformation of society happened because of changes to the modes of production and exchange. As they summarized in *The Communist Manifesto,* "the history of all hitherto society is the history of class struggles" (1998 [1848]: 112). Following this logic, in the emerging capitalist societies of Europe, progress would result from the dialectical relationship between those who controlled the means of production (the capitalist class) and those who controlled the forces of production (the proletariat).

But if the revolutionary moment they called for was near, it was not quite there yet. For that reason, the working classes would have to organize into a political party, "overthrow the bourgeois supremacy" and conquer political power (Marx & Engels 1998 [1848]: 17). However, they were vague about the process of transition to a socialist society (Lane 2021: 457). There was a reference to the dictatorship of the proletariat, but what this entailed exactly was later interpreted differently by a variety of social democrats. This said, Marx made clear that he did not support the idea of a dictatorship. Attacking the anarchists' own version of dictatorship, Marx argued that "no dictatorship can have any other aim than to perpetuate itself, and it can only give rise to and instil slavery in the people that tolerates it; freedom can only be created by freedom […] i.e., by general insurrection and the free organization of the masses from bottom to top" (Marx 1978: 547–8).

While Marx and Engels celebrated the publication of *The Communist Manifesto*, revolutionary activity was bubbling in the streets of Paris. Students, workers and the bourgeoisie took to the streets to demand reforms. King Louis Philippe abdicated and left Paris in disguise, following months of political pressure and social unrest caused by deteriorating economic conditions. In the absence of King Louis Philippe, the people of Paris did not accept his successor to the throne and demanded instead the establishment of a "social republic". It turned out that setting up a "social republic" was not on the cards, as the forces of reaction were powerful enough to put an end to revolutionary fervour. But if radical change was not on the cards, neither was the status quo ante. Universal male suffrage and new civil liberties (including freedoms of the press and of assembly) were established in 1848.

The revolution of 1848 in Paris reverberated across Europe. The news of the events in the French capital soon spread across the continent and similar revolutions took place in Denmark, Switzerland, Poland, the Austro-Hungarian empire, Italian cities such as Milan, Spain and several German states throughout the 1850s and 1860s. It became clear that sooner or later the absolute monarchies of Europe would have to change to accommodate the pressures from below. Fearing radical revolutions that might terminate their reigns, European monarchs offered their subjects new constitutions that limited their own powers. Some of them, namely the monarch in Hungary, went as far as granting the middle classes and workers the right to vote and civil liberties.

But the changes brought about by the "springtime of peoples" (Hobsbawm 1995a: 2) were a far cry from the revolutionary dreams of utopian socialists, communists, anarchists, republicans and anarcho-syndicalists, who formed the resistance against Europe's *ancien régime*. In truth, the debacle of the "springtime of peoples" was a stark reminder of the limited power of the newly formed working-class movements. Many of the revolutionaries of 1848 were imprisoned, whereas others, such as Marx, sought exile in London and suspended their political activism. Marx wrote eloquently about that moment of despair: "After the failure of the Revolution of 1848, all party organizations and party journals of the working classes were, on the Continent, crushed by the iron hand of force, the most advanced sons of labour fled in despair to the transatlantic republic, and the short-lived dreams of emancipation vanished before an epoch of industrial fever, moral marasm, and political reaction" (Marx 1934 [1864]).

If at the time Marx felt despondent about the prospects of a proletarian revolution, European socialists of all guises had reasons to be cautiously optimistic. The seeds of social change had been planted. The labour movement, which expanded because of booming industrial capitalism, was becoming a social and political force to be reckoned with. It soon became apparent that sooner rather than later the *ancien régime* had to give way to an age of constitutionalism in which all working men would have the right to vote and participate in politics.

In response to changed circumstances, some factions of the European left, which at the time was a chaotic gathering of trade unionists, utopian socialists, republican socialists, liberal trade unionists and anarcho-syndicalists, revised their political strategy. Whereas anarchists and utopian socialists continued to refuse to engage with what they regarded as bourgeois institutions, republicans, communists and social democrats followed the instructions of *The Communist Manifesto* and sought to use those very institutions to plot their way into power. Thus, instead of waiting for a new revolutionary moment, which they knew was not around the corner, a new class of socialists aimed to exploit the structures of parliamentary democracy to promote the full emancipation of European workers.

As suffrage was gradually being extended to all male voters across Europe, socialists placed their hopes in political parties which would represent the voices of the working class in the new democratic parliaments. Both Marx and Engels believed that the emancipation of workers could only happen following a revolution which would overthrow capitalism. However, they accepted that the workers' movement had to work with the conditions that existed in society. At that time, parliamentary democracy offered the proletariat a path to conquer political power, which in turn would, as Engels reflected a few years later, pave the way for proletarian rule and "from proletarian rule to none at all" (Engels 1934 [1875]: 340). Similarly, for Marx universal suffrage was a tool that had "the incomparably higher merit of unchaining the class struggle" (Marx 1864).

Working-class politics

The new political activism of the workers' movement was international in nature. Not only was the movement actively engaged in strikes, campaigns and mass protests, but it also started to organize in a transnational manner. In 1864, workers' delegations from a variety of countries, espousing a great diversity of beliefs, met in London and created the International Working Men's Association. Invited to represent German workers, Karl Marx watched the proceedings from a bench in London's St Martin's Hall. He joined the meeting as an interested observer but at the end of it he was elected member of the Assembly's General Council and soon after became its chair (Eckhardt 2016: 1; Smaldone 2020: 70).

Marx was actively involved in the activities of the First International. However, he was pessimistic about what the revolutionary movement of workers could achieve. Indeed, the violent end of the Paris Commune in 1871 dashed any hope of a revolution in the near future. The Paris Commune was a brief experience in revolutionary government which was brutally crushed by the government of Adolphe Thiers after two months in power. The Paris Commune, which ended with the deaths of 20,000 "communards" at the hands of the French army, acquired a mythical status in the imagination of thousands of European socialists and communists. However, it showed, as Jean Jaurès wrote, that "France belonged to the priests, the big landowners and the bourgeoisie" (2022 [1908]: 4).

Marx was equally sobering in his assessment of the Paris Commune. In his essay "The Civil War in France", he argued that "the working class did not expect miracles from the Commune's *decret du peuple*"; they knew that to achieve their emancipation, "they will have to pass through long struggles, through a series of historic processes, transforming circumstances and men" (Marx 1996 [1871]: 188). Because it would take time for the revolutionary moment to arrive and for the workers' movement to achieve political maturity, Marx had advised, the movement "to be *fortiter in re, suaviter in modo*" (bold in matter, mild in manner) long before the defeat of the Paris Commune (Marx 1934 [1864]: 163).

This assessment did not mean that Marx had lost hope in the potential of a workers-led revolution. He simply thought that it would take time for the working class to reach a state of revolutionary readiness. In the meantime, other goals could be achieved through the means that were available at the time. These new circumstances required adapting the strategy of the workers' movement, which should focus on the conquest of political power.[1] The English Chartists and the trade union movement had shown what could be done with the tools available at the time. Without a socialist revolution, they succeeded in bringing about the Ten Hours' Bill. Moreover, a new wave of labour unrest and strikes across Europe demonstrated that the working-class movement was very much alive.

Marx was also aware of his own negligible influence on socialist politics at this time (Hobsbawm 1995a: 114). In truth, the First International was split across three main tendencies. First, there were the communist followers of Marx. Second, there were the followers of Mikhail Bakunin, who led an anarchist tendency that was very influential in southern Europe (Eckhardt 2016: 391). Finally, there was a "socialist" tendency linked to reformist groups (Moschonas 2002: 18). Recognizing that "scientific socialism" was not the dominant trend in working-class politics, Engels explained that "[t]he International was bound to have a programme broad enough to be acceptable to the English Trade Unions, to the followers of Proudhon in France, Belgium, Italy, and Spain, and to the Lassaleans in Germany" (Engels in Marx & Engels 1998: 46–7). Marx also believed that to have any impact, the diversity of the socialist movement needed to be respected, although he expected the different factions to sign up to a programme drafted by him (Eckhardt 2016: 418).

Eventually, the doctrinal diversity, the loose structure and above all the tensions created by the internal conflicts with the anarchist leader Mikhail Bakunin and Marx's own intransigence led to the demise of the international socialist movement. Thus, following the defeat of the Paris Commune and the political repression that soon followed in France, the First International was dismantled. But, as Tony Wright argued, it was exactly in this period that social democracy "became both theory and movement" (1996: 5). It was also around this time that Marx and Engels made peace with the term social democracy. If in the past they had associated social democracy with petty bourgeois values, they were pleased to notice that from the 1870s onwards, social democracy became a Marxist ideology.

From movement to political parties

As the First International slowly dissolved, in Germany the first steps were taken that led to the creation of the first social democratic party in 1875. The creation of the Socialist Workers' Party of Germany (the reference to workers was dropped in 1890) resulted from the merger of two large workers' parties at a congress in Gotha (Guttsman 1981: 44). These two parties, which had emerged in the 1860s, were the General German Workers' Association, which developed under the leadership of Ferdinand Lassalle, and the Social Democratic Workers' Party led by August Bebel and Karl Liebknecht, and which had close ties to Marx and Engels. The latter supported trade unions as a means for workers to assert workplace rights, had a less authoritarian party structure and was more open to the ideas of Marx and Engels (Smaldone 2020: 95).

The choice of the name for the new party was somewhat controversial. Social democracy was still seen as a reformist doctrine. But for August Bebel that formulation was necessary. As he explained in his speech to the Eisenach congress of the Social Democratic Workers' Party in 1869, "we must formulate a programme which is not only socialist but also democratic, otherwise we … cannot expect a solution of the social question" (Bebel quoted by Guttsman 1981: 43). In any case, the party's programme reflected Marxist analysis about the "link between the capitalist system and the dependent status of the worker", referenced the "dictatorship of the proletariat" and stated its desire "to abolish class rule" (Guttsman 1981: 45).

The party counted on Marx's blessing, but that support was not a straightforward affair. In a long diatribe, Marx used his "Critique of the Gotha Programme'" to complain about the undesirable influence of Lassalle and of his "confused bourgeois ideas" about the state, democracy, the capitalist mode of production and its impact on wages. As he put it, "the whole Gotha programme is infested through and through with the Lassalean sect's servile belief in the state, or what is no better, by a faith in the miracles of democracy, or rather it is a compromise between the two types of faith in miracles, both equally removed from socialism" (Marx 1996 [1875]: 224).

Engels shared Marx's reservations. In a letter to Bebel in 1875, Engels wrote that "the State is needed *not for freedom*, but to crush … the *adversaries of the proletariat*" and he suggested that the word "state" should be replaced by "community" or "commune" (Engels 1934 [1875]: 340). And in an irate letter addressed to Bernstein, Engels pointed out that he and Marx had "prophesised the destruction of the state before the anarchists even existed" (Engels 1934 [1872]: 321).

In truth, Marx was vague about the role of the state in the economy and about the concept of workers' control of the means of production. If in *The Communist Manifesto* Marx and Engels defended a centralizing role for the state in the period of the dictatorship of the proletariat (1998: 26), they claimed that once the socialist revolution had succeeded, the state would "die out" because it would no longer be necessary (Engels 1969 [1880]: 147), whereas Lassalle believed firmly in the positive, permanent role of the state in the economy (Guttsman 1981: 45). Interestingly, Marx's conception of the state was largely ignored by future social democrats who adopted Lassalean views of the state.

"Four German socialists": Karl Marx (1818–83) (*top left*), Ferdinand Lasalle (1825–64) (*top right*), Wilhelm Liebknecht (1826–1900) (*bottom right*) and Eduard Bernstein (1850–1932) (*bottom left*)

Source: The Print Collector / Alamy Stock Photo.

The first years of activity of the SPD were extremely challenging because in 1878 the chancellor of the newly unified Germany, Otto von Bismarck, banned the meetings and activities of the social democratic parties as well as the publication of socialist newspapers and pamphlets. He could not, however, remove their representatives from the Reichstag. The ban, known as the Anti-Socialist Laws, lasted until 1891 and aimed to stunt the growth of the SPD. However, in the end those laws were not very effective. By 1891, when the Anti-Socialist Laws were allowed to expire, the SPD was the largest party in Germany attracting 19.7 per cent of the vote (Przeworski 1993: 18). More than that, as the largest European social democratic party the SPD became a model party for other working-class parties around Europe.

The success of the SPD led Engels to reappraise the role of parliamentary democracy in advancing the socialist cause. In "The Tactics of Social Democracy", Engels argued that the SPD had "supplied their comrades in all countries with a new weapon, and one of the sharpest, when they showed them how to make use of universal suffrage" (Engels 1978 [1895]: 565). For him, the franchise had been transformed "from a means of deception into an instrument of emancipation" (Engels 1978 [1895]: 566).

Earlier, Engels used his critique of the Erfurt Programme to explain the democratic nature of the "dictatorship of the proletariat": "if one thing is certain is that our Party and the working class can only come to power under the form of the democratic republic. This is even the specific form for the dictatorship of the proletariat, as the great French revolution has already shown" (Engels 1934 [1891]: 486). It is worth emphasizing that a democratic republic was substantially different from bourgeois democracy. A democratic republic would be led by a workers' party committed to a revolution and to the overthrow of capitalism and the disappearance of the state. This obviously ruled out alliances with bourgeois parties or the dilution of class politics, but equally, it was not a dictatorship as we understand it today.

Varieties of European social democracy

The success of the SPD in Germany had a contagious effect. Soon, similar workers' parties started to emerge across Europe. By the end of the nineteenth century most European countries had a social democratic party. They appeared in Portugal (1875), Spain (1879), France (1879) Norway (1887), Switzerland (1888), Sweden (1889), Belgium (1894), Austria (1898), Finland (1899), Belgium (1894) and pretty much all over Europe. Most modelled their organization and programmes on Germany's SPD (Sassoon 1997: 11). Over time, the social democratic parties of Sweden, Denmark, Norway and Finland developed their own variety of social democracy as they had to adapt to the fact that the industrial working classes were not the majority in their own societies.

In countries such as France, Italy and Spain, workers' parties did not emulate the SPD. Unlike Germany, France did not have a large trade union movement as most industries were organized along small craft lines. In addition, Marxism was not the dominant ideology in French socialist circles. The utopian socialism of Charles Fourier, the revolutionary ideas of Auguste Blanqui and the possibilism of Paul Brousse, as well as republicanism and the anarchism of Bakunin, were equally influential. The result was a heterodox mix which resulted in a divided socialist movement.

In 1879, the Marxists Jules Guesde and Marx's son-in-law Paul Lafargue founded the French Workers' Party, which combined a commitment to the class struggle and the revolutionary overthrow of capitalism as well as "the French revolutionary tradition with its pronounced distrust of organization, strong taste for direct democracy and virulent anti-clericalism" (Sassoon 1997: 12). It was a unique mix that led Marx to disavow Guesde and Lafargue's version of Marxism. In a famous comment to his son-in-law, Lafargue, about the programme of the French Workers' Party, Marx said, "what is certain is that I myself I am not a Marxist" (Marx quoted by Smaldone 2020: 106).

But other and more reformist tendencies joined the party. The moderate "possibilists" were a growing faction, which eventually left the party and launched the Federation of Workers of France. Crucially, the moderate republican and independent parliamentarian Jean Jaurès became an influential voice in social democratic circles and succeeded in unifying the French social democratic movement in the French Section of the Workers' International (SFIO) in 1905.

The heterodoxy and disunity of the French social democratic movement was not exactly an inspiration for other European social democrats. Nevertheless, the French model of the social democratic party was influential in southern Europe, where anarchist and republican ideas among industrial and rural workers and socialist activists were popular. This was also a part of Europe that had not yet developed industrialized economies and solid parliamentary institutions. In Spain, the Socialist and Workers' Party (PSOE), founded in 1879 by Pablo Iglesias, was heavily influenced by Guesdism. In Portugal, the Socialist Party was founded in 1875 and combined in a rather incoherent fashion revolutionary socialists, republicans, liberals and syndicalists (Santos 1983). Similarly, in Italy the Workers' Party, founded in 1892 in Genoa by Filippo Turati and Guido Albertelli, was divided between maximalists and reformists.

Britain, which at the time had the largest trade union movement in Europe, was the great exception to the trend of political organization of the labour movement. Until 1900, when the Labour Party was founded, British social democrats prioritized cooperation with the Liberal Party and proved to be immune to revolutionary temptations. H. M. Hyndman's Democratic Federation (which became the Social Democratic Federation in 1885) had a modest impact on working-class politics. In 1896 William Morris, an eager participant in the European socialist movement, founded the short-lived Socialist League and tried (unsuccessfully) to integrate Marxist ideas into the movement. The Fabian Society, created in 1884, was somewhat more successful. Founded by Sidney and Beatrice Webb and George Bernard Shaw, it campaigned for a reformist approach to socialism, thereby rejecting the Marxist class struggle and revolutionary politics (Shaw 1961). Crucially, the Fabians influenced the revisionism of Eduard Bernstein and the pragmatism of the Dutch Labour Party (PvdA) and became the dominant current within the Labour Party.

When the Independent Labour Party was eventually established in 1893 by the trade union movement, the party was non-Marxist and largely reformist. In truth, Marxism was barely relevant to British socialists. As Ross McKibbin explained, the combination of "pomp and fairness" encapsulated in the Crown and Parliament, together with the patterns of socialization of a highly fragmented working-class movement, a working-class ideology of rights "which was both permissive and restraining" and a party led by workers and not by an intelligentsia explain the weak influence of Marxism over the Labour Party (1984). For these reasons, "the Labour Party was not free to choose between

Marxism and reformism, but only between varieties of reformism" (McKibbin 1984: 331). When the precursor to the Labour Party, the Labour Representation Committee, was finally founded in 1900 by the Independent Labour Party, the Social Democratic Federation, the Fabian Society and crucially the trade unions, what emerged was largely a reformist party which was, in the words of Tony Wright, "not only non-Marxist but anti-Marxist" (1996: 10) and untouched by the doctrinal debates that divided and shaped other European social democratic parties.

The different genealogies of Europe's social democratic parties resulted in different social democracies: some tried to be faithful to Marx, others reflected other intellectual influences and each of them had to adapt to the different political, social, economic, cultural and electoral circumstances in which they operated. But despite the diversity, all social democratic parties shared at the time the broad aspiration to emancipate workers by overthrowing capitalism and abolishing class differences.

An international social democratic movement

Signalling the rise European social democracy as a political force, the Second International was founded in Paris in 1889, the centenary anniversary of the French Revolution, under the active sponsorship of Friedrich Engels. Its first meeting attracted 391 participants from 20 countries, including Russia, Portugal, Britain, France, Germany, Sweden, Austria, Belgium and Greece. Those participants represented social democratic parties, trade unions and socialist propaganda groups. Marxism was the dominant doctrine of all these groups. Its recognized leader was Friedrich Engels, who undertook the mission of promoting Marxism, a task rendered more urgent since Marx's death in 1883. The leading figures of the Second International were Marxists such as August Bebel, Wilhelm Liebknecht, Paul Lafargue, Karl Kaustky, Jules Guesde, Rosa Luxembourg, Clara Zetkin, Georgy Plekhanov and Vladimir Illich Lenin.

But if Marxism was the dominant ideological trend of the Second International, it was not the only one. As Mike Taber explained, there were groups that "still bore traits of pre-Marxist brands of socialism, with a multitude of conflicting perspectives, such as anarchism and syndicalism" (2021: 3). In addition, a rival congress of possibilists was also meeting in the French capital on the same day and attracted a slightly larger number of delegates (567 delegates from 14 countries) although not the most prestigious guests. Indeed, Engels had managed to attract high-profile figures in the European social democratic movement, namely the leaders of the German SPD, Jules Guesde, Edouard Vaillant and Paul Lafargue from France, Eleonor Marx, William Morris and Keir Hardie from Britain, Victor Adler from Austria and Georgy Plekhanov from Russia, as well as some veterans from the Paris Commune and the First International (Taber 2021: 20).

In their first congress in Paris the social democratic movement of the Second International affirmed, in a resolution drafted by August Bebel and Jules Guesde, that the "emancipation of labour and humanity cannot occur without the international action of the proletariat – organized in class-based parties – which seizes political power through the expropriation of the capitalist class and the social appropriation of the means of production" (Taber 2021: 22). By setting this goal the delegates of the Second International established their Marxist credentials. However, they were also pragmatic and strategic in their plan to conquer power.

Aware of the challenge posed by the possibilists, the Second International endorsed their reformist agenda. Thus, alongside a commitment to the overthrow of capitalism through revolutionary means, the Second International was committed to concrete reforms such as the limitation of the working day to eight hours for adults and the banning of child labour, night work for women and of the system of subcontracting. It also recommended the admission women within the ranks of social democratic parties and trade unions and repudiated all wars. The Second International also voted to establish an internationally coordinated day of action on behalf of the eight-hour day. The day that was chosen for demonstrations and strikes was 1 May 1890. This dual approach, which combined long-term goals such as the revolutionary overthrowing of capitalism with short-term reformist proposals, resulted in the triumph of the Congress of the Second International. According to Taber, "within a relatively short time, the Possibilist congress was largely forgotten, relegated to the status of a historical footnote" (2021: 20–1).

With time, social democracy became associated with the radical promise of democracy and the emancipation of the working classes against capitalist exploitation using the institutions of representative democracy and by socializing democracy. In this sense, social democrats were both innovators and realists. They were innovators because they sought to exploit the political and institutional opportunities created by male universal suffrage, and realists because they were acutely aware that a socialist revolution was unlikely to happen any time soon.

The new interpretation of their mission and strategy transformed the nature of the movement. If the participation of workers in democratic institutions transformed bourgeois democracy into social democracy, the participation of social democrats in bourgeois institutions eventually transformed European social democracy. The desire to win elections, and the realization that many workers did not wish to overthrow capitalism, diluted the revolutionary edge from its core commitments.

In the meantime, the term social democracy was no longer used in a derogatory way. By then Engels was fully reconciled with it. He used the 1888 edition of *The Communist Manifesto* to explain why the document had not been called the socialist manifesto. As he put it, "Socialism was, in 1847, a middle-class movement, Communism a working-class movement. Socialism was, on the Continent at least, 'respectable'; Communism was the very opposite" (Engels 1998 [1888]: 48).

Electoralism and doctrinal dilemmas

As social democratic parties wanted to widen their electoral base, they were confronted with the need to adjust their doctrines. Although they were on paper committed to a proletarian revolution, to the class struggle and to overthrowing capitalism, they focused their attention on the pressing problems of the day, namely ensuring that reforms such as the shortening of the working day, or the ban on child labour, were implemented. In addition, social democratic parties became increasingly absorbed by the office politics of parliamentary democracy. These activities left little time to plan the revolution and post-revolutionary society.

The evolution of the SPD is illustrative of these dilemmas. Although it remained committed to the revolutionary goal of overthrowing capitalism, its reformist wing understood that the party could not only rely on the support of the working classes. To grow, the party needed to explore the possibility of attracting the support of peasants and of the professional middle classes. It was the awareness of these factors that led to heated debates following the approval of a new programme at the Erfurt Congress.

The Erfurt Programme of 1891, which was based on drafts prepared by Karl Kautsky and Eduard Bernstein, committed the SPD to the class struggle and revolution and was inspired by Marx's economic thinking. The introduction of the programme was modelled closely on the penultimate chapter of *Das Kapital*, which dealt with the historical tendencies of capitalist accumulation (Guttsman 1981: 72). But the programme also bound the party to pursue reformist goals such as shortening the working week and banning child labour. Kautsky justified such reforms on the grounds that they could strengthen "the suicidal tendencies of the capitalist system" (2021 [1892]: 76).

The approval of the Erfurt Programme did not settle the doctrinal debate within the SPD. Soon after, although not before the death of Engels in 1895, Bernstein published a series of articles in the *Neue Zeit* which suggested a revision of Marxism. Initially Kautsky agreed that some revision was necessary and welcomed his move (McLellan 2007: 25). Thus encouraged, Bernstein noted that, contrary to Marx's prediction, modern capitalism was not leading to a greater pauperization of society and to the concentration of wealth in the hands of a few capitalists. In fact, he argued, Marxism was wrong about two key issues. First, Marx and Engels's "materialist conception of history" was no longer adequate to analyse society because capitalism had changed (Bernstein 2004 [1899]: 20); it was no longer prone to boom and bust or to monopoly (quite the opposite). In addition, Bernstein argued "that the number of the wealthy increases and does not diminish [...] a fact established by the boards of assessment for taxes" (Bernstein 2021 [1899]: 97). The realization that capitalism had developed a structure capable of self-regulation and was therefore no longer contributing to the pauperization of the working classes meant that it could avoid a crisis that was expected to lead to proletarian revolutions.

In a letter addressed to the Stuttgart Congress of the SPD in 1898 Bernstein argued that he had "opposed the view that we stand on the threshold of an imminent collapse of bourgeois society, and that Social Democracy *should allow its tactics to be determined by, or made dependent upon, the prospect any such forthcoming major catastrophe"* (Bernstein 2004 [1899]: 1, emphasis in original). He also noted that the unionized working class was more diverse than conceived by the theorists of socialism: "modern wage-earners are not the homogeneous mass uniformly devoid of property, family, etc, as predicted in *The Communist Manifesto*"; instead, "this 'proletariat' is a mixture of extraordinarily varied elements, of social groups which are even more differentiated than was the 'people' of 1789" (Bernstein 2004 [1899]: 104). In addition, he remarked that "industrial workers are everywhere a minority of the population" and only a small proportion of them took "an active part in working for the socialist emancipation" (Bernstein 2004 [1899]: 106). This analysis led him to dismiss the necessity and likelihood of a revolution followed by the dictatorship of the proletariat (Bernstein 2021 [1899]: 101). Instead of a revolution, he argued that "democracy is a precondition of socialism to a much greater degree than is often supposed. [...] without a certain number of democratic institutions or traditions, the socialist doctrine of our time would be completely impossible. There might as well be a labour movement, but there would be no Social Democracy" (Bernstein 2004 [1899]: 160).

Those were bold claims, but what was perceived as an incendiary provocation was the assertion, inspired by Marx's sentence from "The Civil War in France",[2] that "the final aim of socialism is nothing, but the movement everything" (Bernstein 2004 [1899]: 90). As he explained, "for after all what does it say but that the movement, the series of processes, is everything, whilst every aim fixed beforehand in its details is immaterial to it" (Bernstein 2021 [1899]: 92). Curiously, on this point Lenin agreed: "Marx did not indulge in utopias; he expected the experience of the mass movement to provide the answer to the question as to what specific forms this organization of the proletariat as the ruling class would assume and as to the exact manner whereby this organization would be combined with the most complete and consistent 'conquest of democracy'" (Lenin 1992 [1917]: 37). But, whereas for Bernstein this vagueness led to evolutionary socialism, for Lenin it led, later, to a revolution led by a vanguard party.

Bernstein's attempts to revise Marxism were "vehemently" opposed by Karl Kautsky, the dominant figure of the Second International following Engels's death in 1895, on the grounds they were "theoretically compromised" (Kautsky 2017 [1920]: 170). But despite his vehemence,

Jean Jaurès (1859–1914), who became leader of the French Socialist Party in 1902

Source: AF Fotografie / Alamy Stock Photo.

Kautsky had started to view democracy in a different light and developed a more cautious approach to the prospect of revolution. Indeed, he described the SPD as "a revolutionary party, but not a revolution-making party" (Kautsky 2003 [1909]: 47).

Bernstein's arguments were also loudly condemned by the SPD and by virtually all the parties of the Second International at the Amsterdam Congress in 1904. Bernstein was accused of being too close to Fabian and non-Marxist thinkers. For social democrats such as Lenin and Rosa Luxembourg the commitment to socialist theory was crucial to the movement. Luxembourg had made clear that the role of Marxist theory was to "impose clearly marked limitations to practical activities", thus those who were hostile to theory were mere opportunists (Luxembourg 2021: 69). She was equally adamant about the centrality of revolution. As Luxembourg argued, "the final goal of Socialism constitutes the only decisive factor distinguishing the social Democratic movement from bourgeois democracy and from bourgeois radicalism" (Luxembourg 2021: 3–4). In similar vein, Kautsky argued that what "made anything revolutionary was its end, never its means" (1903). Kautsky's point was a rephrasing of what Liebknecht had claimed earlier at the Erfurt Congress: "What is revolutionary lies, not in the means but in the ends" (Liebknecht quoted by Bernstein 2004: xxvii).

But as Sassoon pointed out, the general condemnation of Bernstein's revisionist thesis "did not reflect the ambivalence many felt towards the orthodox position" (1997: 18). Within the SPD, Bernstein acquired a substantial following among reformists. Hundreds of activists flocked to his public lectures. Trade unionists from other European countries, who at the time were the moderating forces in the Second International, also tended to side with him.

Jean Jaurès offered an interesting halfway stance between these two positions. He argued that democracy offered a more radical power base for the proletariat than a bourgeois revolution. As he put it, "a stronger proletariat no longer has to rely on the favour of a bourgeois revolution" such as those of 1789 and 1848. Instead, the proletariat "has its own organization, its own power", and "has through universal suffrage and democracy an indefinite and extendable legal force" and therefore "he is not reduced to be the adventurous and violent parasite of bourgeois revolutions" (Jaurès 2015 [1901]: 38–9). The truth of the matter was that there was some confusion about the meaning of the concept of revolution: did it imply the need for violence and street fighting or was it a concept that simply described a radical transformation of society? Both Marx and Engels did not have a fixed idea about its meaning, and as a result the concept invited myriad interpretations.

By the early twentieth century, revisionism was an influential trend in several European social democratic parties. Like Bernstein, many of these parties had started to realize that the industrial working classes did not constitute the majority in most European societies. The so-called popular classes also included artisans, small shopkeepers, farmers, self-employed workers, clerks and lower-rank public servants who did not identify with the workers' movement. Social democratic parties realized as well that the unionized industrial working class was not a homogeneous electoral block. This realization led Jaurès to conclude that "if it relies solely on workers, socialism is unable to win" (2015 [1901]: 96).

The recognition of these limits led to a reassessment of electoral strategies. Indeed, the most electorally successful social democratic parties

– for example, Sweden's Social Democratic Party (SAP) – started to broaden their electoral base by targeting the professional middle classes, rural voters and artisans by replacing the traditional reference to the working class with an appeal to the "oppressed classes". Similarly, in Belgium the Parti Ouvrier targeted the professional middle classes, and in Bulgaria, Ukraine and Finland the success of the social democrats was due in large part to the support of rural voters, while in Britain the Labour Party ran for office together with the Liberals.

Another sign of these doctrinal dilemmas was the debate about the prospect of potential collaboration with liberal and bourgeois parties. For most social democratic parties that cooperation was completely out of the question, but it was a difficult dilemma, as the 1898 Millerand Affair[3] demonstrated in France. While Kautsky maintained that the primacy of class struggle precluded cooperating with bourgeois parties, Jean Jaurès and Jules Guesde made the case for broader democratic cooperation. Eventually, in 1900 the Second International passed a compromise resolution leaving the decision to join coalitions with bourgeois parties in exceptional circumstances to the discretion of national parties (Taber 2021: 78–9). However, in 1904, the Dresden–Amsterdam resolution proposed by Bebel, Kautsky and Paul Singer established that "Social Democracy could accept no share in the government within capitalist society" (Taber 2021: 83).

But if electoral considerations and ambitions were slowly shifting the priorities of European social democracy, doctrinal commitments were still very strong. As Sheri Berman argued, the revisionists at the turn of the century "were not yet ready to accept fully the implications of their views and make a clean break with orthodoxy" (2006: 15). Thus, they muddled through, focusing mostly on making concrete proposals that would improve workers' living standards, strategizing the following electoral battles and crucially postponing for another day any debate about the ends of socialism or the revolutionary path to a socialist society.

By 1914, social democratic parties had become key actors in the electoral politics of most European countries, although in most cases they were too small to lead governments. Nonetheless, they played an important role in democratic politics. For example, the French SFIO, which, as Hobsbawm described, "was neither united nor large", elected 103 deputies by virtue of its 1.4 million votes. Similarly, the Italian Socialist Party relied on the support of almost a million voters (Hobsbawm 1995b:

117). In Sweden the social democrats increased their share of the vote from 3.5 per cent in 1902 to 39.1 per cent in 1917. In Norway, the Labour Party went from 0.6 per cent of the vote in 1897 to attracting 32.1 per cent of the vote in 1915 (Przeworski 1993: 19). These electoral results were a mere reflection of how social democrats had centred their electoral strategies on sponsoring practical reforms such as the ten-hour working day and banning child labour, neglecting in the meantime debates about how to develop a socialist society. In the process, social democracy gradually became a reformist ideology.

The collapse of internationalism

Alongside their concerns with electoral strategies, social democrats were more concerned with the prospects of a world war than with a hypothetical revolution and the concrete shape of a socialist society, which Marx and Engels had only sketched out. For them, war and capitalism were intertwined and therefore it was natural that the prospect of war, which was widely debated in the pages of different national newspapers, was a longstanding concern. Indeed, the Second International, a pacifist and internationalist organization, proposed a resolution, drafted by Bebel, Jaurès, Luxembourg and others, which called on socialists to resist war by all possible means. This resolution was unanimously approved at the Stuttgart Congress of 1907 (Taber 2021: 95).

In 1912, when a world war seemed likely, the Basel Congress issued the "Basel Manifesto on War and Militarism" which urged "workers of all countries to oppose the power of capitalist imperialism through international working class cooperation" and insisted "on the demand for peace" (Taber 2021: 142). However, European social democrats were somewhat ambivalent about imperialism. As Eley explained, although enthusiasm for colonialism was rare among socialists, many accepted that it created jobs whereas others believed in the "civilising mission" of European colonialism (2002: 91). Indeed, Bernstein was tolerant of colonialism on the grounds that a "higher civilisation has ultimately higher right" whereas the colonized people had only a "conditional right" to "the land they occupy" (2004 [1899]: 170).

When war broke out in July 1914, most social democratic parties opposed it. They organized anti-war demonstrations and denounced militarism. But soon they concluded that the war was inevitable and that workers supported their governments' mobilization for war. Hence, when the moment came, social democratic parties supported the war efforts of their governments and some even joined them as coalition partners, breaking the commitments made a few years earlier at the congresses of the Second International. However, their support for the war was reluctant and resulted mostly from the fear of losing supporters (Hobsbawm 1995a: 108).

In August 1914, German, Austrian and French socialists supported their governments and voted for war credits. Soon after, socialists in the Netherlands and Hungary adopted "national defensism", as did the socialist parties of neutral Switzerland, Sweden, Denmark (Eley 2002: 125) and the Czech and Hungarian social democratic parties. In Britain, the Independent Labour Party was divided. Whereas the leadership – Keir Hardie and Ramsay MacDonald – opposed the war on pacifist grounds (Hobsbawm 1995b: 108), most Labour MPs supported the patriotic effort. But for leaders such as Jaurès, who was assassinated by a rabid nationalist as the war started, there was no contradiction between the respect and cooperation embodied in socialist internationalism and a commitment to defend the republic against reactionary internal or external enemies (Smaldone 2020: 145).

For the German SPD, the task of supporting the war was rendered more palatable by the fact that Germany would be at war against Russia, a country associated with reactionary values. For party revisionists, such as Edward David and party co-chair Friedrich Ebert, the war represented a great opportunity. They believed social democrats could obtain sweeping constitutional and economic reforms in exchange for their support for the war (Smaldone 2020: 145). But Ebert's stance was not consensual. Karl Kautsky, Rosa Luxembourg and Franz Mehring opposed it.

If the First World War had severely shaken the unity of the Second International, the Bolshevik Revolution of 1917 destroyed it. The doctrinal debates between orthodox Marxists and so-called revisionists about the means and ends of socialism were reawakened and culminated in a profound and traumatic split within the European social democratic family.

Defining revolution

Before the Bolshevik Revolution of 1917, the idea of revolution was a vague but key point in social democratic doctrine. It was a necessary stage on the path to a socialist society, but it was not an imminent one. The revolution could lead to the use of physical violence (*The Communist Manifesto*, written before the revolution of 1848 reached its bloody conclusion, referred to a "violent revolution"), but later Marx had also made it clear that it was not a requirement that applied to all parties; it largely depended on the different countries' state of preparedness, which was linked to the degree of industrialization, the size and politicization of the workers' movement and the existence or absence of democratic institutions.

The concept of revolution was also open to interpretation. It referred to a radical transformation of society which might or not involve violence and street fighting. In his analysis of social democratic tactics, written at the end of his life, Engels explained his reassessment of revolutionary tactics. He did not rule out the use of "street fighting" in the future, but he argued that conditions had changed since 1848, and those were more "unfavourable for civilian fighters and more favourable for the military". By contrast, legal action offered a more effective tactic: "we, the 'revolutionists', the 'overthrowers' – are thriving far better on legal methods than on illegal methods and overthrow", he argued (Engels 1978 [1895]: 571).

Echoing Engels, Kautsky argued that "the contrast between a reform and revolution does not consist in the application of force in one case and not in the other" (1903: 7). Therefore, as he argued in *The Class Struggle*, "it is by no means that it [the revolution] be accompanied with violence and bloodshed" (2021 [1892]: 74). Instead, he argued that "revolutions are the result of slow, gradual development (evolution)" (Kautsky 1903: 16), and did not require violence. At the time, Lenin was equally cautious and gradualist in his approach to revolution. As he argued, "if Social Democracy sought to make the socialist revolution its immediate aim, it would assuredly discredit itself" (Lenin quoted by Sassoon 1997: 19). Eventually the Bolshevik Revolution of 1917 forced a clarification of this debate.

The prospect of a revolution in Russia had been debated among the different socialist leaders and intellectuals since at least the 1870s. By then, and following the failed revolutionary moves of 1905, it was clear that the Tsarist regime was on its knees. However, there was a consensus among Marxists, including Lenin, that Russia was not ready for a Marxist proletarian revolution.

But it is one thing to make a cool and rational assessment from a comfortable distance; it is quite another when political actors face moments of political instability and popular insurrection that create opportunities for revolutions. When the Menshevik provisional government fell in October of 1917, Lenin, who had returned from exile in Switzerland in April, did not waste the chance to seize power. Indeed, the Bolshevik party seized power in Petrograd on the 7 November (25 October in the Gregorian calendar). On the following day, the Bolsheviks took control of the Winter Palace and issued a series of decrees – known as Decrees on Land – whereby private property was abolished and land was distributed among the peasants. But as Hobsbawm explained, "the new regime did little about socialism except to declare that this was its object" (1994: 63).

These developments were followed closely by European social democrats. Overall, they were supportive of the Bolshevik Revolution. But that support was reversed when it became clear that Lenin and his comrades had renounced parliamentary democracy and were responsible for the repression of thousands of Russians. It had been some time since Kautsky had concluded that "the only form of the state in which socialism can be realized is that of a republic, and a thoroughly democratic republic at that" (2003 [1909]: 47). Thus, when he was confronted with the facts of the Bolshevik Revolution, he claimed that "their dictatorship" was a "contradiction to the Marxist teaching" as it did "not appear to be a transitory emergency measure" but "as a condition for the long duration" (1988 [1918]: 103). Kautsky's comment was consistent with Marxism. In a letter addressed to Bebel, Liebknecht, Bracke and others, Marx had warned that "[w]e cannot therefore co-operate with people who say that the workers are too uneducated to emancipate themselves" (Marx & Engels 1934 [1879]: 377).

Other European social democrats agreed with Kautsky's reappraisal of the concept of revolution. The Austro-Marxist Rudolf Hilferding remained committed to the idea of revolution, and even accepted the prospect of a temporary dictatorship of proletariat, but argued that, in contrast with the Bolshevik experience, which was predicated on a government of a party elite, he argued that "the emancipation of the working class must be its own work" (2017 [1920]: 328). Similarly, the French socialist leader Léon Blum warned his party comrades about the stifling uniformity and lack of democracy and freedom of thought that Lenin wanted to impose on the international socialist movement and argued that the main difference between the socialism of the SFIO and Leninism was not about revolutionary principles. The main difference was about democracy. He also stressed that while French and European socialists understood revolution as "a transformation of the economic regime", Lenin's conception was about "an armed struggle against a bourgeois power" (Blum 2016 [1920]: 96).

Lenin on the other hand was no longer eager to ally himself with bourgeois parties such as the social democratic parties of Europe.[4] For him, social democrats were "present-day traitors to socialism" (Lenin 1992 [1917]: 42). Thus, on seizing power in Russia, Lenin changed the name of the Russian Social Democratic Labour Party to the Communist Party of the Soviet Union and took steps to create a disciplined internationalist movement that would aggregate all genuine revolutionary parties.

In 1919 two rival international congresses took place which, as Taber explained (2021: 145), codified the split of the socialist family. In February, a Congress in Bern officially reconstituted the Second International, which was now very different from the one founded by Engels in 1889. A month later, a rival congress met in Moscow and founded the Third International, also known as the Comintern (Taber 2021: 145–6). In contrast with the Second International, the 21 conditions for membership, which had been drafted by Lenin and Grigori Zinoviev, were strict. They established that communist parties had to draft their programmes in conformity "with the special conditions of the country" and "the resolutions of the Communist International" (Sassoon 1997: 35).

As a result of the schism, communist parties emerged across Europe, often following secessions from social democratic parties, and joined the Comintern. In Germany, the Bolshevik Revolution led to the emergence of three socialist parties: the Majority Social Democrats, the Independent Social Democrats and the Spartacus League dominated by Luxembourg and Liebknecht. French and Italian socialists hesitated about staying in an SPD-dominated Second International. Following the warning made by Léon Blum about the undemocratic nature of the

Third International, the SFIO rejected the 21 conditions at a party congress in Tours. However, in a consequential move for the SFIO, most party activists voted to join the Comintern. Across Europe, other social democratic parties, many of which had participated in wartime governments, now wished to continue operating within the parliamentary framework. They were committed to reformism and attacked the Bolshevik Revolution, in particular its use of terror and rejection of parliamentary democracy (Smaldone 2020: 165).

This schism, which had been looming for some time, provoked a crisis within European social democracy. Practically everywhere in Europe the socialist movement was divided between social democrats who were now doctrinally committed to democracy and communists who defended proletarian revolutions led by a vanguard party.

The democratization of social democracy

In the first 50 years or so of its existence, social democracy underwent a profound transformation. If, in the 1870s, social democracy lost its bourgeois and obscure reputation to become a hugely influential Marxist movement committed to socialist revolution, by the 1900s social democracy had become a political force to be reckoned with in European politics. Along the way, social democracy lost its revolutionary edge and became strongly involved in electoral politics. By the 1920s, European social democracy was defined by its commitment to the parliamentary road to socialism and by its vehement rejection of violent revolutions and of the dictatorship of a vanguard party as a long-term goal. Consequently, social democracy became associated to a conception of revolution understood as a form of "radical transformation" of economic systems of production as well as reforms that made capitalism palatable to the working classes but also to the professional middle classes and swaths of rural voters. To some extent these changes were the result of trying to apply socialist doctrines to countries with different political traditions and economic structures. The new social democratic parties had to adapt to the realities that their participation in democratic politics created; they improvised and added their own interpretations to vaguely defined principles through processes of layering and drifting, but they were also forced to respond to two big external shocks: the First World War and the Bolshevik Revolution.

On paper, some social democrats still defended a socialist revolution understood as a radical transformation of society, and most were committed to the overthrow of capitalism and private property as a route to achieve the emancipation of the working classes. Thus, the first revisionism was one that asserted the centrality of democracy and defended a parliamentary road to socialism. But as Chapter 2 shows, choosing this path to socialism opened the way to further revisions of social democratic doctrine.

2

Social democracy embraces capitalism

As European social democracy responded tentatively to the challenges posed by Soviet communism, fascism, the economic depression of the 1930s and the trail of destruction a new world war left across Europe, it went through a new transformation in its second act. This transformation was neither rapid nor straightforward. By processes of drift and layering, but also in response to big external shocks, European social democrats slowly revised their doctrine, programmes and practices.

Having settled on a parliamentary path to socialism, which now required the development of diverse electoral coalitions and relied on potential tactical alliances with bourgeois parties, they now had to reflect on social democracy's approach to capitalism. That process of revisionism started as a pragmatic and ad hoc response to immediate economic and political crises and electoral pressures, but by the 1950s it became a new doctrine, which revised the means of social democracy.

To chart this second phase in the history of European social democracy, this chapter explains how social democratic parties and intellectuals responded to the varied and challenging crises of the 1920s and 1930s, namely the rise of fascism and economic depression. Next, the chapter analyses how the economic consensus that emerged at the end of the Second World War set the stage for the revision of social democratic doctrine. The final section of the chapter charts how the end of the postwar consensus in the 1970s placed European social democracy on the defensive again. Along the way, the chapter explores variations in the practice of social democracy across Europe.

The interwar period: responding to different crises

The interwar years were disorientating because they brought European social democrats closer to political power (in some cases – in Germany, Austria, Britain and Spain – into government), but ultimately, they became distanced from the goal of emancipating workers through revolution and the overthrow of capitalism. The truth was that this was not an easy time to lead governments or to participate in electoral politics. The threat of fascism, the emergence of communist parties that competed for the same voters as social democratic parties and the Great Depression were big challenges to which European social democracy was ill-prepared.

In the few cases where social democrats found themselves in power, they entered government without a roadmap that led to socialism. In truth, Marxist analysis had accurately described capitalism's proneness to boom and bust, but it offered scant advice on how to deal with capitalist crises. This was deliberate. As Kautsky explained, it was pointless to draft detailed plans when the conditions of the future were unknown. As he put it, plans that proceeded from suppositions instead of facts were "fantasies and dreams which remain[ed] at best without result" (Kautsky 2021 [1892]: 103).

But without a plan they did not know what to do when the capitalist economy hit the buffers as it did in 1929. The influential theoretician of the German SPD Rudolf Hilferding promptly admitted to this shortcoming when he said that "we find ourselves in an age in which real changes have outstripped scientific understanding" (Hilferding quoted by White 1981: 255). Eventually, and because they wanted to win elections, the social democratic parties that were in power became slavish followers of the balanced budget.

Moreover, choosing the parliamentary road to socialism required other adjustments, namely coming to terms with the actual voting behaviour of workers and doing some basic electoral arithmetic. This entailed recognizing, as Bernstein had suggested, that not all working-class voters dreamed of a socialist revolution and accepting that voters' behaviour was driven by a variety of factors including their emotions. In *The Psychology of Socialism* (1927) the Belgian socialist intellectual Hendrik de Man argued that reason was not central to most people's worldview and behaviour. Instead, he emphasized the importance of irrational and emotional sentiments in people's behaviour, and he suggested that the deeply embedded nationalism exhibited during the First World War proved to be a more powerful driver of voting behaviour than class consciousness. For those reasons he believed that social democratic parties should appeal to people's emotions and focus on concrete policies whose effects could be felt immediately (Smaldone 2020: 184). The Austro-Marxists were equally well attuned to the force of nationalism. Noting the national upheaval within the multinational Austro-Hungarian empire, Otto Bauer warned that the "national disposition" of the working class endangered "its unity and class-consciousness" (2017 [1909]: 36).

European social democrats also had to adjust to the requirements of governing in the challenging political and economic circumstances that followed the end of the First World War. In Germany, the SPD led the government during the tumultuous period of 1918–20, which culminated in the replacement of the constitutional monarchy by a parliamentary democracy (proclaimed by the majority Social Democratic Party) that became known as the Weimar Republic. At this specific time, the SPD was cast, as Guttsman argued, "in the role of midwife to the institutions of a liberal democracy" (1981: 311).

But this was a highly turbulent period. Alongside setting up new political institutions, Germany had to deal with the costs of losing the war and in particular the punitive terms of the Treaty of Versailles (1918), which in turn led to widespread political polarization and social deprivation but also to a major constitutional transformation. The political atmosphere was so charged that many felt that Germany was on a verge of a revolution (Eley 2002: 165), although, and with the benefit of hindsight, Sassoon argued that "few of the preconditions for a German version of the Bolshevik Revolution existed" (1997: 48).

To make matters worse, the social democratic movement was bitterly divided between the leadership of the SPD, which prioritized a smooth transition to parliamentary democracy over a socialist revolution, the pacifist Independent Socialists of the Independent Social Democratic Party of Germany (USPD), which defended a middle way between reformism and Bolshevism, and the communist Spartacist League, which proposed following the Bolshevik model.[1] These divisions culminated in the violent repression of the Spartacist League and the assassination of its leader Karl Liebknecht and of the charismatic intellectual Rosa Luxembourg on 15 January 1919. Their deaths and the elections to the National Assembly in 1919 marked a turning point in German politics. The SPD won 37.9 per cent of the vote but did not control a majority in the Reichstag and ended up forming a coalition government with the Centre Party and the German Democratic Party.

These electoral results were a big achievement, but the political situation was far from ideal because the SPD had to compromise on a programme of government. While the SPD-led government was able to enact a democratic constitution that established universal suffrage and basic civil liberties, and introduced some social reforms such as the eight-hour day, unemployment benefits, an institutionalized system of wage regulation, the expansion of social insurance and housing reforms, it left the conservative institutions of the German state intact. The civil service, the military and the judiciary remained unreformed and pursued, with the blessing of the SPD, a policy of repressing revolutionaries (Lindemann 1983: 226; Sassoon 1997: 49).

This was also a period when important debates within the German and Austrian social democratic parties took place, and which had far-reaching implications for social democratic doctrine. The Austro-Marxist intellectual who became the leading intellectual of the SPD and Germany's finance minister, Rudolf Hilferding,[2] argued that capitalism had entered a new phase of development. Instead of being competitive and crisis-prone, capitalism was being transformed by the growing role of the state in managing the economy (Hilferding 2017 [1930]: 739). In similar vein, Otto Bauer claimed that "Manchester liberalism is dead" because "all economic organizations seek to place the state in their service" (2017 [1909]: 33). In light of this transformation, Hilferding proposed an "organized capitalism" that implied "*the fundamental replacement of the capitalist principle of free competition with the socialist principle of planned production*", which also involved "transforming the capitalist organized and managed economy into one guided by the *democratic state*" (Hilferding 2017 [1927]: 572, emphasis in original). In short, the Austro-Marxists argued that capitalist development would shift to what Bauer called the "equilibrium of class forces" between the bourgeoisie and the proletariat. This in turn, would, in the words of Max Adler, reduce the "sharpness of class conflict in favour of a politics of compromise" (2017 [1926]: 450).

Faced with a new form of capitalism as well as with the realization that not all workers aspired to a socialist revolution, German social democrats engaged in debates about the aims of the SPD. Revisionists such as Bernstein urged the SPD to become a *Volkspartei* (a people's party) and to declare itself the party of the working people (a term that encompassed all workers and not just industrial workers). This was a cunning reading of the possibilities created by universal suffrage, but the move was rejected by the party. Kautsky was still the SPD's leading theoretician and he managed to convince the party to reject Bernstein's proposals. As an alternative, he turned to Otto Bauer's theory of the balance of class forces (Berman 2006: 99).

The difficult economic circumstances and the constraints of governing in a coalition also shaped debates about economic policy. By 1923 the experience of high inflation convinced social democrats "that once the currency had been stabilized, no tampering with it of any sort could ever be allowed again" (Lindemann 1983: 231). Between 1925 and 1928 a group of party economists led by Fritz Naphtali tried to shift the terms of the debate. They proposed to set up what they defined as economic democracy that included nationalizations, industrial democracy, central cooperative institutions and a national wages policy (Smaldone 2020: 182). But these proposals were resisted by both the SPD-led government and by those who interpreted them as a revisionist move.

Instead of economic democracy, the finance minister, Rudolf Hilferding, called for a more restrictive monetary policy and tax rises and opposed expansionary policies aimed at boosting employment and production. He was also convinced that "capitalism will not collapse as a consequence of its own contradiction" (Hilferding 2017 [1930]: 769). Hence, when the depression hit Germany in 1929, leading to a steep rise in unemployment, the SPD implemented public-spending and wage cuts and rejected proposals to reflate the economy through public investment, although eventually it resigned from the government in March of 1930 (Guttsmann 1981: 321). The socioeconomic situation was so desperate, and the political landscape was so unstable, that by 1933 the Weimar Republic had collapsed and Adolf Hitler was appointed German chancellor, with the Nazi party controlling a third of the seats in the Reichstag. By the end of the decade, Nazi Germany had occupied most of Europe. By then, as Sassoon explained, the SPD realized that its first experience of a "parliamentary road to socialism" had been "inauspicious" because the reconciliation between capital and labour had failed (1997: 52).

The Austrian social democrats experienced similar challenges but followed a different path. For Otto Bauer, the leading figure of the SPÖ, the choice of a different path was deliberate, as he believed that the German SPD had drifted too far to the right (Lindemman 1983: 248). As leaders of a coalition government the Sozialdemokratische Partei Österreichs (SPÖ) focused its energies on establishing the democratic republic of Austria (which was no longer the headquarters of the now defunct multinational Habsburg Empire) and on organizing elections in the newly reconfigured country, but they had not forgotten their ideological goals. At the end of the First World War, the SPÖ was dominated by its left wing, which promised a middle way between reformism and Bolshevism (Leser 1976: 137). In practice this meant that the Austrian social democrats rejected membership of the Comintern, but they were committed Marxists who believed in the collapse of capitalism and in the socialist revolution.

Their new understanding of the workings of the capitalist economy meant that they were more committed to reforming capitalism from within than to overthrowing it. In truth, they seemed to be aware that some revisionism of social democratic doctrine was taking place. In any case, Renner justified this revisionism on the grounds that "seen through the eyes of Karl Marx, today's world is completely different than the historical analogies from past centuries allow it to appear" (Renner 2017 [1930]: 823) and for that reason "the road to socialism is via the state" (Renner 2017 [1930]: 819).

However, their doctrinal commitment to Marxism was not sufficient to secure a lasting popular mandate at the country's first democratic elections. The SPÖ's first experience in government was in coalition with the Christian Socialists. But a disagreement about the appointment of advisers for the armed forces triggered the collapse of the coalition government and eventually led to the start of the civil war (Eley 2002: 226). At the time the Austrian social democrats felt that they had laid the first foundations of the parliamentary road to socialism, and left a lasting impact in Vienna, which the SPÖ controlled. They had introduced several important social reforms, namely the eight-hour week, paid holidays for workers, the reduction of child labour and night work for women and the establishment of a comprehensive system of healthcare and social insurance (Leser 1976: 139). But the sense of achievement did not last long. The socioeconomic achievements of the SPÖ in Vienna and other parts of the country governed by social democrats provoked huge resentment in the more conservative parts of Austria. By 1927, tensions between the social democrats and Christian socials reached a peak. On what became known as "Bloody Friday" there were violent confrontations between right-wing paramilitary organizations and workers' military organizations. At the 1930 elections, the SPÖ was the most voted party, but by 1933, and following the Nazi takeover in Germany, the balance of political forces changed (Lindemann 1983: 250-1). By 1934, Austria was led by a fascist government.

In Britain, the Labour Party was growing fast. As the party's membership doubled, in 1918 the Labour Party adopted a socialist platform drafted by the Fabian Sidney Webb, which predicted the collapse of capitalism in Europe, the gradual introduction of democratic socialist control of the country's means of production and promised, in the famous Clause Four, "to secure for the workers by hand or by brain the full fruits of their industry and the most equitable distribution thereof that may be possible upon the basis of the common ownership of the means of production, distribution and exchange".

The steady rise of Labour's popularity convinced the party's leadership to seek independence from the Liberals. By 1922, Labour had supplanted the Liberals as the second largest party in parliament. Therefore, when the Conservatives lost their majority in 1923, Labour was in position to lead a government, which they did from 1924. Because it did not control a majority, the party had to rely on the support of the Liberals to govern. But Liberal conditions were not Labour's main challenge. Its big problem was Chancellor Philip Snowden, who was, in the words of Laybourn, "impeccably orthodox in his economic thinking" and who therefore believed that "socialist policies could only be financed out of a budget surplus" (2013: 19). Indeed, Snowden rejected the expansionary policies proposed by Liberals such as David Lloyd George and John Maynard Keynes (Laybourn 2013: 19–20) but also by Hugh Dalton, a Fabian party member and economist (Mudge 2015: 74), and endorsed instead the conservative orthodoxy of the British Treasury.

Consequently, Labour's first government, led by Ramsay MacDonald, was unable to implement any of the socialist measures contained in its manifesto such as the nationalization of the mines, railways and electric power stations, although it managed to approve an ambitious programme of investment in public housing. In truth, MacDonald told voters that "he foresaw the introduction of socialism only as a very distant project since the country's economic conditions and the mentality of the population did not yet permit it" (MacDonald quoted by Lindemann 1983: 236). Despite Labour's moderation, the government collapsed after nine months in power. Labour seemed poised to win the 1924 elections, but four days before the election, the infamous and fake Zinoviev Letter was published. This letter, which falsely revealed Labour's alleged plans to launch a communist revolution, sealed the party's electoral results.

Labour returned to power in 1929, a period which coincided with the Great Depression. Unsurprisingly, MacDonald was eager to show that Labour governments were responsible with public finances. Thus, instead of implementing countercyclical measures to tackle the deep recession, the Labour government adopted the Treasury orthodoxy of balanced budgets and monetary stability. MacDonald and Chancellor Snowden were so committed to this course of action that "it was only a Cabinet revolt which prevented the 1929–31 government from cutting financial assistance to the unemployed" (Padgett & Patterson 1991a: 9). Unable to deliver the policies that its supporters wanted and forced by conventional wisdom to implement economic policies which failed to prevent a recession, Labour obtained disastrous results at the 1931 election. This defeat left Labour in an electoral and doctrinal quandary: if British voters were not prepared for full socialism, they were equally unimpressed with a Labour government that governed in the same way as the Conservatives.

While in Germany, Austria and Britain social democrats cooperated with bourgeois parties, French social democrats remained faithful to the approach of the Second International which ruled out such coalitions. More seriously, the socialist movement was suffering from the schism of the Second International. At its Tours Congress in 1920 the schism became official when many party members seceded to form the French Communist Party (PCF), which joined the Comintern. This schism had considerable electoral consequences as the French socialists lost thousands of supporters to the communists. To stop the haemorrhage of supporters, the leaders of the SFIO felt the party had to reaffirm its revolutionary socialist credentials. Part of that strategy involved the continued refusal to cooperate with bourgeois parties (Colton 1953: 520).

In the meantime, the leader of the SFIO, Léon Blum, tried to navigate the challenging times as best as he could. It was only after the socialists' defeat in 1919 that the party changed its stance regarding coalitions with bourgeois parties. By 1924 the SFIO cooperated with the Radical Socialists and emerged as the second largest left-wing party in the country. The "one-minute" electoral pact to form a "cartel des gauches" (a left-wing cartel) in parliament enabled a government led by the Radical Socialists, but it stopped short of becoming a coalition government (Judt 1976: 205). Even though this was a compromise, the SFIO was uneasy with this solution.

It was during the period of 1925–6 that Blum developed his ingenious approach to cooperation with "bourgeois" parties. In a series of speeches and articles, Blum claimed there was a difference between the "exercise" and the "conquest" of power. Whereas the "conquest" of power was the prelude to "revolutionary transformation", the "exercise" of power within "an existent capitalist regime" was a consequence of "class action under its political and parliamentary force" (Blum 2016 [1946]: 139). This distinction paved the way to participate, under specific conditions, in governments with other parties. These conditions were (1) possessing a majority in parliament and (2) being the strongest party in a parliamentary coalition. Blum also insisted that if those conditions were met the party would participate in government, but only if it led it. Blum's ingenious proposals were approved by the party, despite opposition from the Guesdist wing.

In 1929 Blum's thesis was tested. The leader of the Radical Socialists, Edouard Daladier, offered the SFIO the opportunity to join his government. Those who argued in favour of joining this coalition were able to get a resolution approved at the party's congress whereby the socialists agreed to participate in a government if exceptional circumstances, which were left unspecified, were met. Those exceptional circumstances emerged in the 1930s. The economic crisis, the Stavisky affair,[3] the growing Nazi threat, the attempted right-wing coup against the republic and growing political instability became the "exceptional circumstances" that could justify socialist participation in a bourgeois government. In 1934, the socialists announced that, if necessary, they would participate in a coalition of republican defence (Colton 1953: 527).

Soon after this announcement, the government of the Popular Front was announced with the goal of protecting the republic from fascism and addressing the effects of the economic crisis. The decision to participate in the Popular Front paid off handsomely. At the 1936 elections, the three parties of the Popular Front – the Socialists, the Radical Socialists and the Communists – were the winners. More importantly, for the first time in the history of the French Republic, the Socialists were the largest party in the chamber and were now able to lead a government (Colton 1953: 527). Blum's thesis was vindicated, and he became prime minister in a coalition government with the Radical Socialists (the Communists refused to join the coalition but supported the government). The government only lasted two years but was able to approve an impressive amount of socialist labour legislation (Colton 1953: 528).

In Italy, the Italian Socialist Party (PSI), which emerged from the war as the strongest political party, was unable to use its electoral popularity and the climate of social unrest to lead a socialist revolution (Berman 2006: 102). In truth, the party was deeply divided into factions. There was a reformist faction that defended an evolutionary socialism, a maximalist faction that remained wedded to the pre-war Marxist orthodoxy, the communists led by Amadeo Bordiga and a "culturalist" faction around the figures of Antonio Gramsci, Angelo Tasca and others (Sassoon 1997: 73). Eventually, in 1921, Amadeo Bordiga, Antonio Gramsci and their associates decided to secede from the PSI to create the Italian Communist Party (PCI).

These ideological conflicts had a disastrous effect on the party's electoral prospects. As workers occupied land, organized direct action in factories and organized strikes, lower-middle-class and middle-class voters were growing scared of the social unrest that did not seem to abate. In the end, they turned to Benito Mussolini and his fascist party, which promised order, stability and prosperity. By 1922 Mussolini was prime minister and a year later he changed the electoral law which enabled him to win the 1924 elections.

In the Iberian Peninsula, social democracy was subsumed in heated national debates about republicanism, modernity and, in the case of Spain, revolution (Aviv & Aviva 1981). In Portugal those debates culminated in the collapse of the First Republic in 1926 and in the establishment of authoritarian rule, whereas in Spain the debates escalated into a civil war that culminated in the collapse of the Second Republic in 1936. By the end of the 1930s fascist-inspired authoritarian regimes led Portugal and Spain until the mid to late 1970s.

The experiences of the German, Austrian, British and French social democratic parties in government at the time of the depression of the 1930s tested their ideological commitments. The experience of governing and pursuing electoralism had transformed social democratic leaders. In his famous theory of the "iron law of oligarchy", Robert Michels (1966 [1911]) suggested that social democratic leaders no longer seemed open to new ideas and had instead become bureaucratic and more interested in power than in revolution. But if European social democratic parties in government seemed to lack imagination, a range of alternatives to capitalism and communism began to be sketched out by committed but reformist social democrats. These alternatives represented a form of revisionism because they sought coexistence with capitalism, but it was a revisionism that was still committed to the final ends of socialism.

The Swedish exception

The Swedish social democrats were the first to experiment with alternatives to communism and capitalism but only after choosing a more pragmatic road to socialism. The SAP had started life in 1889 as an emulator of the German SPD, adopting the orthodox Marxism of its Gotha Programme, but soon it carved out a different and more pragmatic path which was better suited to Sweden's economic and social circumstances, and also to new economic and social conditions which had been unforeseen by Marx and Engels. Thus, the SAP's take on Marxism was undogmatic (Berman 2006: 153; Tilton 1992).

Before the First World War, the SAP, led by the former journalist Hjalmar Branting, was already unambiguously committed to a parliamentary road to socialism and focused its strategy on proposing reforms that would ameliorate workers' living and working conditions. The party was also aware that in Sweden there was no proletarian majority. To grow electorally, the party had to attract the support of middle-class voters and peasants. But winning the support of those voters required a different electoral strategy based on a programme that did not scare the property-owning middle classes and peasants (Esping-Andersen 1988:

21). The SAP then decided to adopt a programme that was consistent with this electoral goal.

This pragmatic choice paid off. By 1917, the SAP had gained widespread support among workers and was willing to share power with bourgeois parties. In 1917 it joined a coalition with the Liberal Party. By 1920, the party abandoned the policies of balanced budgets it had pursued earlier and carved up instead a successful alternative to economic liberalism and Bolshevik economic planning. The new alternative was presented in the party's new programme which stressed "the need for economic planning" and proposed taxation "as the means by which collective production would be financed" (Lindemann 1983: 253).

The success of the SAP is often explained by its doctrinal pragmatism. The Swedish social democrats sacrificed doctrinal purity for the sake of electoral success (Tilton 1992: 410). But the SAP's discarding of Marxism does not mean that Swedish social democracy was not principled or that it has not made important contributions to the theory of social democracy. In many ways, Swedish social democrats were the early pioneers of the revisionism that became the norm within social democratic parties in the postwar period, and which entailed a strong commitment to a tamed form of capitalism as well as to equality, democracy and solidarity.

The authors of Sweden's social democratic economic policy were Ernst Wigforss and Gustav Möller, two creative economists who presented economic growth as the condition to provide for the needs of all. Wigforss was a revisionist thinker who argued that the role of social democracy was not to overthrow capitalism but instead to transform bourgeois society by democratizing the power of capitalists. As Tilton explained, "Wigforss was a revisionist, but not a revisionist who had struck a truce with capitalist society" (1979: 506). In fact, he was drawn to some of the new economic ideas coming out of the United Kingdom, in particular the works by English radicals and Guild Socialists (who inspired his proposals for economic democracy). But his most important contribution was his proposal to address the severe economic crisis with countercyclical measures such as stimulating aggregate demand (Berman 2006: 169).

His ideas can be described as Keynesianism before Keynes, as allegedly he developed and implemented his policies four years before Keynes published his *General Theory* (Tilton 1979: 508). Przeworski maintains that "it remains a matter of controversy whether the Swedish policies were developed autonomously, from Marx via Wicksell, or were already an application of the already circulating ideas of Keynes" (1993: 36; Bergström 1992: 143), but it is undeniable that in the same period the economists of the Stockholm School, and in particular Gunnar Myrdal, were reaching similar conclusions to those of Keynes (Mudge 2018: 136–7) and proposing the same countercyclical policies in response to the economic crisis.

Another key figure was Per Albin Hansson, who became party chair in 1928 and transformed the SAP into a catch-all party. To that end, he borrowed from the right the idea of a "people's home" or *folkhemmet*. By this he meant a conception of society where "equality, consideration, cooperation and helpfulness prevail" (Hansson quoted by Tilton 1992: 411–12). In practical terms, the idea of *folkhemmet* centred on three key features: agricultural price supports, a countercyclical full employment

Per Albin Hansson, 1945

Source: Archive PL / Alamy Stock Photo.

programme and a programme of social reform (Esping-Andersen 1992: 44; Tilton 1992: 404). The SAP's "people's home" approach was astute because it enabled the party to develop a catch-all electoral strategy. When the Great Depression hit Sweden, the party used the idea of *folkhemmet* to tell voters its programme was directed not only at industrial workers but to anyone who needed support from the state (Tilton 1992: 411).

While social democrats were floundering across Europe, in Sweden they had an impressive breakthrough in 1932. As a minority party, they were able to negotiate a coalition with the Farmers' Party. It was from this period that SAP put in place its transformative social democratic policies (Molin 1992). This move was courageous but appropriate. In the period 1932–3 the economic crisis had thrown a third of Sweden's workforce into unemployment and led to violent confrontations (Judt 2007: 364).

In response to the crisis, Wigforss made the case for increased public spending to offset the lack of private investment, promote full employment and address the threats of depression. Such a course of action was justified by the belief in the capacity of governments to stabilize the economy and promote full employment. Alongside these measures, Wigforss introduced progressive taxation to fund a comprehensive welfare state and put in place original ideas of economic democracy, which empowered workers.

In addition, the Swedish social democrats were the first to develop a systematic theory which proposed the reversal of the class struggle in sequential order (Esping-Andersen 1988: 22). Whereas an orthodox Marxist approach assumed that socialism could arise only after the socialization of production, Swedish revisionism held the view that political and then social reforms could create the conditions for economic transformation, step by step (Esping-Anderson 1988: 22). Thus "political citizenship" preceded "social citizenship", which were indispensable to the third stage: "economic citizenship". This approach assumed that workers had to be emancipated from social insecurity before they could participate effectively in economic democracy. On the other hand, economic democracy allowed workers the possibility of participating in the organization of economic activity (Tilton 1992: 411).

This innovative economic approach, which spared Sweden from the mass unemployment and deprivation experienced in most European countries in the 1930s, meant that the SAP emerged at the end of the Second World War as a trusted and popular party, which had developed its own brand of social democratic politics. The SAP's approach was based in the development of a tamed form of capitalism which involved public investment in public infrastructure, the prioritization of full employment, a generous welfare state funded by progressive taxation and economic democracy but that, unlike the social democratic parties in Germany or Britain, rejected public ownership. The rationale to reject nationalizations (which the party had defended in the 1920s as a means to achieve equality) was that economic democracy was a more practical and effective way to achieve social justice (Esping-Andersen 1992: 38). This was a perfectly reasonable argument, but it is also true that the opposition parties of the right launched a successful campaign against nationalizations (Sassoon 1997: 158).

In 1944, the Swedish social democrats were ready to revise their programme. The previous but vague Marxist analysis and references to the class struggle that had survived earlier reforms were replaced by general statements of principles that committed the party to "transform the economic organization of bourgeois society" and to place "the rights of determination over production" in the hands of the people" (Bergström 1992: 144–5). Interestingly, the policy tools creatively developed by the SAP in the interwar period would become mainstream in the postwar politics of western Europe.

The postwar consensus

A new politics emerged in Europe out of the ruins of the depression of the 1930s and the Second World War (1939–45). The need to reconstruct European countries and to prevent the re-emergence of fascism led west European politicians to adopt a radically different approach to the economy. Crucially, the United States emerged from the war as the leading superpower in the West and, having orchestrated with the Soviet Union the division of Europe along ideological lines (with eastern Europe succumbing to the Soviet line), it seemed determined to prevent the spread of communism into western Europe. To that end, the Truman administration launched the defensive military North Atlantic Treaty Organization (NATO) and made a substantial contribution to

European reconstruction through the generous Marshall Plan. Because the United States had an interest in demonstrating that capitalism resulted in prosperity for all, the Marshall Plan enabled the adoption of a radically different approach to the economy.

The other impactful geopolitical change was the launch of a project of European integration, which sought to prevent a new war in Europe and whose first foundational steps were the creation of the European Coal and Steel Community in 1951 and of the European Economic Community in 1957. These projects aimed to first create a single market in Europe and later to unify the continent in a federal union. The project started modestly with six member states (including, crucially, France and Germany), but over time it transformed the European continent.

However, the emerging new consensus was not an exclusive social democratic invention. Many of the instruments that defined that post-war consensus, such as Keynesianism, owed more to Liberal thinking than to socialist ideas (although, as we saw, the Swedish social democrats had pioneered a new approach to crisis management). The same can be said about the welfare state, whose first foundational stones had been placed by Liberal and Conservative politicians but further developed by social democrats (Hobsbawm 1994: 272). It is also worth recalling that the so-called social democratic consensus was heralded, almost everywhere, by governments of the centre-right. With the exceptions of Britain, Sweden and Norway, social democrats were in opposition in the immediate decade following the end of the Second World War. In this period, newly formed Christian democratic parties, which supported the mixed economy and the welfare state, gained ground and were in direct competition with social democratic parties. These parties proved to be particularly popular in Germany, France, Austria and Italy.

The implications of the new geopolitical and electoral reality meant that social democrats had either to "catch-up" with the new conventional wisdom or to propose something more radical. Most chose to do the former. Across Europe social democrats were ready to endorse the new postwar consensus around a reformed capitalism and the welfare state. Gradually but unevenly Keynesianism[4] became the new social democratic economic orthodoxy, to which they added robust welfare states. The Great Depression had taught social democratic parties that the doctrine of balanced budgets had deepened the recession. Emboldened by the example of Sweden, European social democrats, together with conservatives and Christian democrats, were ready to defend a more robust role for the state in economic affairs. Full employment became a goal pursued by parties of most ideological persuasions as well as planning (in some form) the expansion of the welfare state and public ownership of the means of production.

For social democrats, Keynesianism offered simultaneously a lifeline and an existential crisis. It was a lifeline because demand management aimed to tame capitalism's cycles of boom and bust and secured, at least at the beginning, high rates of economic growth, high wages and full employment. But Keynesianism challenged social democratic doctrines. Its adoption implied that social democrats were no longer committed to the destruction of capitalism. Instead, the endorsement of Keynesianism meant that the social democrats were tying their chances to the success of a different type of capitalism.

In some cases, this distinctive capitalism entailed economic planning. The planning ideas that gained currency in the 1950s had enjoyed some popularity among socialists in the interwar period. German and British trade unions, Bertrand de Jouvenel's *Economie Dirigée*, published in 1928, and Britain's Guild Socialists had been toying with planned economy ideas that aimed to offer an alternative to Bolshevism and market capitalism (Pels 1987: 208). Perhaps the most popular and influential ideas on planning were put forward by the Belgian socialist intellectual Hendrik de Man in 1934.

For the Belgian Workers' Party, de Man's plan seemed to offer a solution to its doctrinal crisis as it offered an alternative to Marxism, reformism and national socialism (Pels 1987: 207) as well as a plausible response to the economic depression. In practical terms, planning entailed a mixed economy, whereby banks and key industries were to be reorganized as public services (although not necessarily owned by the state). Planning, of course, entailed the acceptance of private property and a free economy to counterweight the threat of statism. The purpose was to – as the "planist" slogan put it – develop "a strong state which could tear down the wall of money" (Pels 1987: 223–4).

In the 1930s de Man's ideas were dismissed for being too close to fascism (Judt 2007: 68), but in the postwar period they regained popularity, although they remained vague and attracted different interpretations. These ideas came to encapsulate the view that the state would perform a key role in the economy, including controlling key industries and deciding industrial policy. For example, in France "planning" was embraced with great enthusiasm by the political class and not only by social democrats in the form of industrial policy, whereas in Britain it was presented as the nationalization of industries and nothing else (Hobsbawm 1994: 272). By contrast, the Italian socialists rejected nationalizations because of its closeness to fascism (Judt 2007: 71–2), whereas in Sweden social democrats separated "ownership" from "control" and preferred the latter to the former. The reason for this was that it was preferable to regulate and control private companies than to absorb the inefficiencies and costs that public ownership would entail (Przeworski 1993: 38).

Swedish social democrats were also defenders of economic democracy and consequently implemented a series of policies aimed at giving more power to workers. Indeed, part of the Swedish social democratic blueprint involved the 1951 Rehn–Meidner model, which combined active labour market policies (to retrain and compensate workers who had lost their jobs) with a system of solidaristic wage bargaining (Esping-Andersen 1992: 52) and aimed to keep inflation in check and promote full employment, high wages and greater equality. The German SPD adopted a similar approach. For them, the "socialization of the economy, meant the restructuring of big industry but not full nationalizations" (Padgett & Patterson 1991a: 14). However, the SPD was in opposition until the late 1960s and was unable to implement any of its policies.

Thus, there was some variation in the way European social democrats perceived the role of the state in the economy and in how they interpreted policies aimed at socializing and democratizing it. But there was one area of consensus: European social democrats were in favour of the expansion of the welfare state and almost universally, although with some variation in terms of scope, defended more robust protection for the unemployed, offered health care coverage and argued for the development of social housing, higher investment in education and more robust systems of social insurance and pensions.

Sweden developed the most extensive and generous welfare state that would be funded by progressive taxation, but Britain was not far behind. The Attlee government followed the recommendations of the Beveridge Report, which was published in 1942 and became an instant bestseller, and set up a National Health Service funded by taxation to provide healthcare to all free at the point of delivery, extended unemployment and retirement coverage and sickness allowance, invested in public housing and nationalized industries such as the railways, public utilities and mines as well as, crucially, the Bank of England.

While adopting Keynesianism, planning and nationalizations, and developing generous welfare states, which in themselves resulted in the radical transformation of European societies, European social democracy started, almost without noticing it, a period of revisionism in the postwar period with its economic policies increasingly distant from Marxism. The class struggle had been replaced by electoral strategies that sought to attract the support of different social classes, and opposition to capitalism metamorphosed into accommodation.

This electoral pragmatism reflected changes in the composition of social democratic parties. Stephanie Mudge's *Leftism Reinvented* (2018) shows that parties such as Britain's Labour Party, Sweden's SAP and Germany's SPD underwent a consequential organizational transformation throughout the twentieth century. If in the late nineteenth century party intellectuals (many of them self-taught) drafted electoral programmes, by the 1950s, trained economists led those parties' programmatic changes that resulted in the adoption of a more technocratic language in its rhetoric and programmes. Mudge's analysis of party programmes demonstrates that these three parties, together with the American Democratic Party, "converged on a shared language that was nonsocialist, strikingly optimist, and distinctively economistic" (2018: 50). According to Mudge, this reflected the fact that party experts tended to be distanced from the membership, were more attuned to the aspirations of a wider electorate and "tended to be at odds with union leaders and credentialed economists" (2018: 6). If their expertise resulted in some electoral victories and policy success, they nonetheless lacked, as Berman argued, "the old-timers' hunger, creative spark, and theoretical sophistication" (2006: 188). This transformation was eloquently described by Anthony Crosland: "Today we are all incipient bureaucrats and practical administrators. We have all, so to speak, been trained at the LSE, are familiar with Blue Books and White Papers and know our way around Whitehall. We realise that we must guard against romantic or Utopian notions" (2006 [1956]: 404–5).

This change, as well as the move leftward experienced by centre-right parties, led intellectuals such as Daniel Bell and Seymour Martin Lipset to declare the "end of ideology" in a series of essays published in the late 1950s. Both Bell and Lipset argued that democratic politics and the socioeconomic achievements of the postwar consensus had left the main political parties merely disagreeing about technocratic aspects of public policy. However, this ideological convergence was consequential for social democracy, as social democratic parties gradually abandoned the still existent but faint revolutionary zeal that had survived the revisionist battles of the early twentieth century and developed a new revisionism which transformed the means of social democracy.

Embracing capitalism

The adoption of Keynesianism, planning, nationalizations and the welfare state as the instruments of social democratic politics represented a significant revision of social democratic doctrines. Indeed, instead of being committed to the overthrow of capitalism and to a classless society, social democrats were adopting the policy tools that made capitalism palatable to the working classes and the poor and socialist ideas acceptable to the middle classes. More than that, the adoption of the mixed economy and the welfare state ensured the survival of capitalism. This meant that social democrats could no longer claim that over the long term capitalism would eventually disappear. However, in the immediate postwar period social democrats still paid lip-service to the anti-capitalism that had animated the movement, but, as Moschonas argued, "this was mere nostalgia" (2002: 21).

This programmatic shift was visible in the activities of the recently reconstituted Socialist International. In 1951, the Socialist International declared that socialism "aims to liberate the [world's] peoples from dependence on a minority which owns or controls the means of production", "to put economic power in the hands of the people as a whole, and to create a community in which free men work together as equals" (Smaldone 2020: 223). To a certain extent the vagueness of the definition reflected and enabled some diversity in the practice of social democracy across western Europe.

This definitional vagueness was important because the revisionism of social democratic doctrines did not happen at the same time in different social democratic parties. Several factors affected that change, namely the different responses to the depression and their war experiences, as well as the presence or absence of strong communist parties. As explained earlier, in Scandinavia – particularly in Sweden – that change had been happening since the 1930s and was relatively smooth. In Austria there were changes, but a residual commitment to Marxism remained. In countries such as France and Italy, which had strong communist parties, the socialist parties were reluctant to engage in revisionism, although it must be said that both the SFIO and the PSI were more heterodox in terms of doctrine than the SPD had been (Zariski 1962: 373). In Britain, the Labour Party adopted the postwar consensus with ease, but there was some debate around the question of the democratization of the economy. The Fabian-dominated Labour Party remained committed to the principle of common ownership of the means of production and adopted a paternalistic approach to the state.

There was equally some debate about the ends of socialism. In 1956, Anthony Crosland published *The Future of Socialism*, which had the ambition to revise the Marxist doctrine that prevailed in European social democracy more as a piece of furniture than as a practice. In this work, Crosland noticed the radical transformation of capitalism which had falsified "without exception" Marx's prophecies (Crosland 2006 [1956]: 4). Reflecting Bernstein's observations made at the turn of the twentieth century, Crosland argued that "the belief that the 'inner contradictions' of capitalism would lead to a gradual pauperization of the masses, and ultimately to the collapse of the whole system, has by now been rather obviously disproved" (2006 [1956]: 5). Echoing Hilferding's arguments of the 1930s, he noted that the business class had "lost its commanding position" and in its place the state had gained political authority over economic decision-making, namely in the promotion of full employment, the rate of economic growth, balance of payments and the distribution of incomes" (2006 [1956]: 9). In short, capitalism was a very different beast from the one theorized by Marx and Engels.

The changes were so profound that Crosland declared that the historical definition of capitalism no longer applied to the British economy (2006 [1956]: 33). This realization led Crosland to promote a socialism that was to be defined by its "ends or ideals" and which for him were a cooperative aspiration, a commitment to equality and welfare but which would renounce some of the traditional socialist means, namely public ownership (Crosland 2006: 77–88). In particular, Crosland claimed that the economic power of the bourgeoisie no longer needed to be the centrepiece of social democracy's struggles, because the separation of ownership and control eliminated that problem.

Crosland was not the only one seeking to revise Labour's doctrine. Following from Crosland's attempts to "revise" socialist doctrines, the Labour leader Hugh Gaitskell tried, in the period 1959–60, to revise Clause Four of the party's constitution. This was a totemic paragraph which committed Labour to public ownership, and which had become, in the words of Tony Wright, the "ideological glue to hold together the assorted worshippers" (1996: 126). But the revisionists' attempts failed, leaving Labour's practice further disconnected from its theory until 1995, when Clause Four was eventually revised.

Similar debates took place within the French SFIO. Léon Blum and other like-minded reformists made the case for change, but their attempts to broaden the party's appeal and abandon its revolutionary commitments fell on deaf ears (Sassoon 1997: 133). In the postwar period the SFIO abandoned many of its traditional stances, although its programme remained committed to Marxism. To some extent, the SFIO's resistance to revisionism was shaped by electoral considerations. On the one hand, the PCF was a formidable force and attracted considerable support from working-class voters; on the other hand, the Gaullist Party was committed to reforming capitalism. As a result, the party suffered from programmatic paralysis, which in turn stymied French social democrats' attempts to develop a distinct and electorally successful programme.

In Germany, the process of doctrinal revisionism only started in the 1950s. Then, dissatisfaction with the party's electoral failures culminated in the adoption of a new programme at the Bad Godesberg congress of 1959. This programme committed the SPD to reform capitalism and to a people's party strategy that sought to attract voters beyond the traditional industrial working class (Padgett & Paterson 1991b). Famously, the programme of Bad Godesberg committed the party to promoting "as much competition as possible, as much planning as necessary" (SPD 1959). In addition, the party "no longer considered nationalization the major principle of a socialist economy but only one of several (and then only the last) means of controlling economic concentration and power"[5] (SPD 1959). Perhaps more dramatically, the new programme claimed that "democratic socialism, which in Europe is rooted in Christian ethics, humanism and classical philosophy, does not proclaim ultimate truths" (SPD 1959).

This commitment to humanism and Christian ethics meant of course the relinquishing of the idea of class struggle. At a stroke, the Marxist roots of the party were erased, and the SPD became a "volkspartei", that is, a people's party. Similarly, the party's commitment to pacifism was eliminated as the SPD now supported NATO membership and Germany's rearmament, as well as membership of the European Communities (EC). According to Moschonas, these changes turned the SPD into "one of the most right-wing social democratic parties in the European socialist family of the era" (2002: 57).

The SPD's Bad Godesberg Programme came to symbolize social democracy's new revisionism, which fully embraced capitalism and was merely committed to reformism, the improvement of living standards, social mobility and the reduction of poverty. European social democrats remained committed to equality and a reformed capitalism, but they came to accept inequality. This revisionism sought to transform the electoral fortunes of social democratic parties, although its immediate results were paltry. By the 1960s European social democrats seemed exhausted, despite many social democratic parties being in power. In Italy, the PSI joined a centre-left coalition government in 1963. A year later, Britain's Labour Party returned to government after 13 years in opposition. In Germany, the SPD joined a Grand Coalition with the Christian Democratic Union in 1966 and then headed its own government for the first time in 1969. In Finland, Social Democrats and Communists formed a Popular Front government in 1966, whereas in Sweden, Denmark and Norway, social democrats were almost hegemonic political forces (Eley 2002: 364). In 1971, the Austrian social democrats won an absolute majority at the parliamentary elections. But despite this renewed electoral strength, social democratic parties had lost energy and enthusiasm. Part of the problem was that social democratic ideas were now part of the new political consensus.

An emerging social Europe

Above all, the transformation of social democratic parties meant that they were totally unprepared for the wave of contestation and protests that hit western Europe in the late 1960s. One of the fruits of the social democratic consensus of the postwar period was a very large student population who were not happy with the status quo. Young Europeans were worried with the deterioration of the environment, persistent racism, gender inequality and class differences. Thus, the 1960s was a period in which feminist, anti-Vietnam war, anti-racism and environmentalist activists took to the streets, started university occupations, engaged in imaginative forms of direct action and demanded radical change. The student protest movement was particularly notorious in Paris in 1968, but youth contestation was happening everywhere. Left-wing intellectuals, in particular those who moved in the circles of the New Left, the Frankfurt School and French existentialist circles, debated the intellectual sterility and managerial capture of social democratic parties, attacked consumer culture and demanded more democracy and true emancipation.

In parallel with youth protests, western Europe experienced a new wave of industrial unrest. In a few cases, such as in France in 1968, students protested alongside trade unionists. In other countries trade unions organized strikes in search of higher pay and better working conditions. By the end of the 1960s social unrest was widespread. Deteriorating economic conditions and the threat of unemployment led to a new wave of strikes in Norway, Denmark and Italy and to lesser extent in the Netherlands, Belgium and Finland (Sassoon 1997: 357–63).

Some social democrats embraced the new emerging culture. They supported feminist causes, such as the legalization of abortion and the public provision of childcare, and endorsed green ideas to protect ecosystems from industrial pollution and nuclear weapons. Equally, some social democratic parties responded to workers' demands. In France the SFIO embraced *autogestion,* which was the French take on economic democracy or co-determination, while in Sweden and Denmark the social democratic governments extended economic democracy as a way to compensate workers for wage restraint. The Danish Social Democrats approved a model of economic democracy in 1969 which aimed to develop "a more democratic and socially responsible economy" and a fairer distribution of wealth (Esping-Andersen 1988: 302). Inspired by the Danish experience, the Swedish social democrats proposed the addition of wage-earner funds to the Rehn–Meidner programme. These wage-earner funds gave trade unions the right the participate in

Meeting of the European Social Democrats in Hamburg, West Germany, 1980. Olof Palme, Bruno Kreisky and Willy Brandt (*top row, left to right*); Anker Jorgensen, Joop de Uyl and Helmut Schmidt (*bottom row, left to right*)

Source: ZUMA Press, Inc. / Alamy Stock Photo.

companies' decision-making, redirected company profits into collective funds and protected workers from unfair dismissal.

Worried by deteriorating economic conditions and sensing that economic change was in the air, the leaders of Germany's SPD (Willy Brandt), Austria's SPÖ (Bruno Kreisky) and Sweden's SAP (Olof Palme) debated the "future of social democracy" and suggested that its survival depended on the deepening of economic democracy and on a renewed commitment to the transformation of society. As Palme proposed during his dialogue with Brandt and Kreisky, "the essential component of democratic socialism, consists in achieving democracy in all areas of society" and in creating "forms of democratic labour and one democratic community" (Brandt *et al.* 1976: 36). Kreisky agreed with Palme's proposal and argued that the condition to achieve democracy at all levels is to "give to the greatest possible number of people access to information and to codecision" (Brandt *et al.* 1976: 56). Brandt in turn justified the focus on economic democracy and codecision on the grounds of creating countervailing power to the growing might of multinational corporations (Brandt *et al.* 1976: 143).

Because he understood that the challenge to workers' working conditions and freedom was global, Brandt presented his proposals, which had been influenced by the work of the transnational group of socialists in the European Parliament (EP), to strengthen economic democracy and Europe's social dimension to his partners in the EC (Shaev 2020). Under his impulse, and with the support of the French government, the EC started to develop a social dimension to the European project. As Aurélie Andry explained, the aim of this loosely defined project was "to renew socialism" at the European level in order to address some of the demands raised by the new social movements and to use "the EC to strengthen control over capital beyond the national level" (2022: 11). To that effect, in the early 1970s the EC considered a range of proposals, including the development of tools "for a policy oriented towards a new distribution of all wages and income" and towards "guaranteed employment and harmonized social security" which would be "achieved in collaboration with workers' and employers' organizations and embodied in the 'European social budget'" (Andry 2022: 126). The European Commission, headed by Sicco Mansholt, proposed the creation of a mechanism to guarantee workers' incomes when facing economic changes created by European common policies and suggested that "social Europe" was a precondition to Europe's monetary union (Andry 2022: 126–7). Crucially, in the late 1970s, the commissioner Henk Vredeling presented what became known as the Vredeling directive, which proposed employee participation in the management of multinational companies (European Works Council), namely of its profits and capital growth (Andry 2022: 222).

But by the end of the 1970s most of the EC's "social agenda" was either severely watered down (as in the case of the Vredeling directive)[6] or abandoned. The deteriorating economic situation created by the oil shocks and rising inflation, disagreements between social democrats, trade unions and communist parties, and a change in the leadership of the SPD condemned those plans to history (Andry 2022: 221). The new SPD leader, Helmut Schmidt, supported by the British Labour prime minister, James Callaghan, believed that Keynesianism had run its course and a new era of fiscal rigour was needed, while the Swedish social democratic government was ousted in 1976, and as result the proposals for wage-earners' councils were heavily diluted (Esping-Andersen 1988: 300) and eventually abolished in 1992.

The end of the postwar consensus

By the late 1970s it became clear that the postwar social democratic consensus had started to unravel. The collapse of the Bretton Woods system, the oil shocks, the rise of inflation and stagflation tested the limits of the Keynesianism. Without economic growth the state did not have the capacity to redistribute wealth, invest in public services or stimulate the economy. Social democrats soon realized that it was no longer possible to rely on the compromise formulas of the postwar period and were forced to confront what Padgett and Paterson called the "'malign syndrome' of stagnation, inflation, rising unemployment, a spiral of state debt, and trade imbalance" (1991a: 155).

At the time, social democrats were in power in Norway (1971), Sweden (until 1976), Denmark (1971), Germany (1969), Austria (1970), the Netherlands (1973) and Britain (1974), but the challenging economic circumstances meant that their approach to governing was managerial and uninspiring. That managerial approach was particularly visible in Germany where the new chancellor, Helmut Schmidt, focused on demonstrating that the SPD was a responsible government.

In Italy, the PSI followed the trend for programmatic revisionism of European social democracy although in its own idiosyncratic fashion, that is to say, after ideological fusions and splits (Rizzi 1974). By 1970, the moderate and astute leader Bettino Craxi set aside the Marxist doctrines that had dominated the party and adopted a cautious reformist veneer. But it still took more than a decade for the modernizing effort to be rewarded at the ballot box. The Communist Party, led by Enrico Berlinguer, was still the strongest left-wing political force in Italy and had captured the imagination of European left-wingers with its "Eurocommunism"[7] (Di Donato 2015). It was only in 1983 that Craxi became the first socialist prime minister in Italy.

The French SFIO followed a similar revisionist trajectory. Predictably, successive electoral defeats drove the process of reform. By 1971, the SFIO was dismantled and different socialist factions founded the French Socialist Party. But despite the modernized image, the French socialists retained their left-wing profile, which was visible in the winning platform deployed by François Mitterrand in 1981 as well in their willingness to form an alliance with the Communist Party. Mitterrand won the 1981 presidential election with a distinctly social democratic programme. However, soon after being elected he had to reverse gear.

In the new democracies of southern Europe, socialist parties, which followed the French model of social democracy, became important players. In Spain, the PSOE won the 1982 elections and was in power for more than a decade. Greece's Panhellenic Socialist Movement (PASOK) won the country's second democratic elections in 1981 and established itself as a party of government. In Portugal, the Socialist Party won the first elections of democratic Portugal in 1975 and quickly became a party of government. Crucially, the socialist parties of southern Europe emerged as moderate and revisionist parties: defenders of NATO membership, proponents of membership of the EC and resigned to a "remedial" conception of social democracy.

In Britain, the British Labour Party was forced to confront the new economic realities of high inflation, industrial strife and a deteriorating economic outlook. By 1976, James Callaghan acknowledged that Keynesianism had run its course. As he put it in a speech to the Labour Party: "We used to think that you could spend your way out of a recession and increase employment by cutting taxes and boosting Government spending. I tell you in all candour that that option no longer exists" (Callaghan 1976). The crisis of social democracy was felt even in the Scandinavian countries where it had been most successful. As Esping-Andersen explained, at the time social democracy seemed "at best, exhausted; at worst, dying" (1988: 318).

The implications of revisionism

The second of act of European social democracy was defined by a new transformation (or revisionism) of the means of social democracy. The proposals for economic democracy made in the 1970s showed that European social democrats were still committed to the goal of human emancipation in a society shaped by fraternity and cooperation. However, by supporting the survival and success of a revised form of capitalism, social democratic parties accepted too that inequality would not be totally eradicated. In the meantime, they tried to innovate and adapt traditional social democratic goals to new circumstances. By responding to external shocks, and through processes of layering (especially the stimulus programme adopted during the 1930s recession, the development of welfare states and the promotion of economic democracy), drift and displacement (the gradual abandonment of the goal to overthrow capitalism), social democracy was transformed into a reformist ideology committed to improve the living conditions for working people and the vulnerable within the structures of a capitalist economy. Nonetheless, social democrats still argued that the state could regulate and reform capitalism with the purpose of achieving socialist ends.

That transformation was at first tentative and incremental, but by the late 1950s it seemed irreversible. The embrace of capitalism, the ditching of the last remnants of Marxism from their programmes, the technocratic takeover of social democratic parties and the crisis of Keynesianism left social democratic parties ideologically disorientated. If they remained committed to the aspiration of more equal societies, they did not know how to achieve it. Nonetheless, in this second act European social democracy had managed to reform capitalism in ways that were compatible with some social democratic aims. What social democrats did not foresee was that the economic crisis of the 1970s would make them reassess their belief in the capacity and desirability of the state to reform capitalism. When that reassessment finally took place in 1980s and 1990s European social democrats enabled the dilution of the ends of social democracy.

3

Riding the Third Way wave

In a familiar pattern, the third act of social democracy was defined by crisis, revisions and retreats. Faced with new demographic, political, economic and electoral challenges, European social democrats decided that the only way to survive as a political force was by diluting (this does not mean abandonment) their commitments to social justice and equality and accepting the primacy of markets over politics (Berman 2006). In short, social democrats stopped believing in the ability of the state to regulate the market with the purpose of achieving social democratic aims. The acceptance of monetarism and of the European Union's (EU) neoliberal turn privileged the pursuit of low inflation through a monetarist approach which entailed a commitment to fiscal discipline, which in turn required the retrenchment of the welfare state and the acceptance that inequalities may rise and that full employment may not be achieved. The nature of this revisionism was so encompassing that many analysts, scholars and activists wondered whether there was anything left of the European left.

To fully understand the third big transformation of European social democracy, the chapter starts by briefly outlining the political and economic context that led to it. Next, it identifies the three key factors that shaped the transformation of European social democracy in the 1990s, namely, demographic changes to the composition of the electoral coalitions of social democratic parties, globalization (and in particular the liberalization of international trade) and the triumph of neoliberalism, the neoliberal turn of the EU and the identity crisis triggered by the collapse of communism in the Soviet Union and in eastern, central and Baltic Europe.

Next, the chapter charts the development of the new revisionism, popularly known as the Third Way, by outlining its main traits and analysing the debates among party intellectuals and the programmatic shifts that most social democratic parties underwent in this period. The chapter explains that this Third Way wave was not uniform across Europe, although, paradoxically, it contributed to a convergence of social democratic practices across the continent. Finally, the chapter shows that although initially it was spectacularly successful at the ballot box, by the early 2000s the Third Way wave started to crumble, paving the way for a new existential crisis of social democracy.

New revisionist winds

Although social democratic parties were in power in several European countries throughout the 1980s, the spectre of an existential crisis haunted them. Sweden, Austria, France, Spain, Greece and Italy were among the rare countries where social democratic parties were in power. However, the type of social democracy they practised was highly diluted. Instead of investing in public services and in the welfare state and promoting economic democracy, social democratic governments felt constrained by globalization. As Scharpf explained, the impact of globalization left social democrats without a clear strategy "to adapt national economies to the constraints of the international capital markets" (1987: 249). Eventually, social democratic parties accepted the demands of markets and adopted tight rules on public spending, liberalized and reformed labour markets and reformed welfare states with a view to make them leaner. The sense of disorientation and malaise provoked by these changes was so acute that over the decade intellectuals such as Alain Touraine (1983), Ralf Dahrendorf (1980) and others prophesized the death of socialism.

The French Socialist Party (PSF) became the paradigmatic case of the dilemmas social democrats struggled with at the time. In 1981, the PSF led by François Mitterrand won the presidential and legislative elections on a radical programme, which was designed to be shared with the Communist Party and other parties of the left. This programme included a Keynesian approach to macroeconomics which privileged full employment and an ambitious programme of nationalizations. But the deteriorating economic situation, the growth of the public deficit and public debt, the devaluation of the franc and the threat of capital flight placed France in a precarious position. In 1983, and under pressure from the bond markets and the German government, Mitterrand announced his "tournant de la rigueur" (austerity turn), which implied the end of the socialists' radical agenda and the enactment of monetarist policies. Jacques Attali, a former socialist minister and a friend of the French president, said that Mitterrand was torn between choosing European construction or social justice. Eventually he chose the European project (Attali quoted in Lordon 2001: 118) over social democratic values.

The choice was stark because the European Monetary System devised by the German social democrat Prime Minister Helmut Schmidt and the centre-right French President Giscard D'Estaing reflected ordoliberal[1] values which imposed severe constraints on the ability of national governments to decide their macroeconomic policy. Under these plans, member states had to keep their national currency within the parameters of the Exchange Rate Mechanism.[2] In the case of France, this meant that the socialist government had to pursue a strong franc policy, which undermined the government's ability to pursue a Keynesian approach to full employment.

The French socialists were not the only ones to be asked to make this choice. The Spanish, Portuguese and Greek socialist parties faced a similar dilemma. In Spain, the PSOE won four consecutive elections between 1982 and 1993, but that electoral triumph was achieved at the expense of ideological coherence. The Marxist identity that had shaped the PSOE in the mid-1970s was downgraded at an extraordinary congress in 1979 (Kennedy 2009: 95) where the party embraced a "modernization agenda" that aimed to adapt Spain's economy to the requirements of EC membership. Instead of nationalizing some industries or promoting full employment, the PSOE government introduced monetarist anti-inflationary policies and prioritized the interests of the business sector over those of workers in the new fiscal policies and in the new investments in infrastructure and skills it implemented in 1980s (Recio & Roca 2001: 178). Nonetheless, the Spanish Socialists were able to substantially strengthen welfare provision to Spanish citizens.

In Greece, PASOK, which had won a landslide victory in 1981, underwent a similar process of economic "modernization" along European lines, although it remained rhetorically committed to social democratic policies (Tsakalotos 2001: 141). In Portugal, where the transition to democracy was accompanied by substantial political instability and economic crises, the Socialist Party was not in power for long, and when it was it had to implement austerity policies to comply with the International Monetary Fund interventions in 1978 and 1983.

In Italy, the PSI under the leadership of Bettino Craxi started a process of reform in 1981 which involved the major decision to dissolve its ties with the PCI with which it had collaborated at the municipal level (LaPalombara 1982: 929). The PCI, which was still the second largest party in Italian politics and the leading representative of "Eurocommunism", was hopeful that the historic compromise between the communists and social democrats would endure. But the PSI was determined to take a separate path, a resolve that became more acute following the violent assassination of the Christian Democrat prime minister Aldo Moro by the terrorist anarchist group Red Brigades in 1978, which, incidentally, had no links to the PCI (Sassoon 1997: 586).

The dissolution of ties with the communists was a bold move considering that the PSI was at the time the smallest social democratic party in Europe, while the Italian PCI was a much stronger political force. However, the impact of this decision was unequivocal. Craxi's reforms meant that the PSI had expunged the last drops of residual Marxism from its programme and assumed a liberal-socialist identity. At the Palermo Congress in April of 1981, the PSI adopted "The Theses", which committed the party to "pragmatism, gradualism and reform" (LaPalombara 1982: 932). These new values were expressed in the rejection of nationalizations, in the support for the privatization of some national companies and in a commitment to welfare state retrenchment.

As the PSI carved a pragmatic path to power, the popularity of the Italian communists declined, especially following the collapse of the Berlin Wall in 1989. However, as explained later in the chapter, in the mid-1990s there was an unexpected turn of events which resulted in the emergence of a new left-wing force out of the ashes of the PCI, which nonetheless confirmed the identity crisis of European social democracy.

Sweden's SAP did not escape this reformist trend. Following an electoral defeat in 1976, the social democrats underwent a process of programmatic reform which tried to respond to the challenges of globalization. The SAP's 1981 programmatic revision, entitled "Third Way", promised budgetary discipline, a commitment to low inflation and a range of supply-side reforms that included liberalization, fiscal reforms, the promotion economic competitiveness over equality, the acceptance of the partial privatization of some public services and a new approach to wage policy (Tsarouhas 2009: 115; Åmark 1992: 435). This final change resulted in the watering down of the Rehn–Meidner model, which was Sweden's flagship progressive model of economic democracy. In Norway, social democrats struggled to recover from the electoral losses experienced in the 1970s, although they remained in office for most of the period but mostly as partners of coalition governments.

For the social democratic parties that remained in opposition for most of the 1980s, the rightwards shift happened at a slower place. For example, in Britain, following an electoral rout in 1979, the party embarked on a leftwards drive under the leadership of Michael Foot, which resulted in a traumatic defeat in 1983. It was only from 1987, and following the party's third consecutive defeat, that the party led by Neil Kinnock and Roy Hattersley announced a Policy Review. In the party document *Meet the Challenge, Make the Change*, Labour not only embraced the market economy but promised to run it better than the Conservatives. Kinnock also introduced organizational reforms that resulted in the weakening of Labour's National Executive Committee and granting greater autonomy to the leadership (Shaw 1994: 114–15). But Kinnock's reforms did not result in electoral victories. Labour lost the 1992 election, the party's fourth consecutive defeat since 1979.

Similarly, the German SPD was divided about its strategy following its defeat in 1983. Immediately following that defeat the party moved to the left. But soon after that it opted for a policy of "co-operative opposition" and eventually, in 1989, it adopted a new "basic programme" (known as the Berlin Programme), which replaced the Godesberg Programme of 1959 (De Deken 1999: 92–3). This programme represented an accommodation to new social and economic realities but still asserted the party's social democratic and working-class roots (Pautz 2009: 133). The party's ambivalence was also visible in its approach to European integration. The programme affirmed the belief in a federal Europe and a "fair world economy", but the left was critical of the single market and had doubts about the plans to launch a single currency (Hertner 2018: 69). In the end, the party had little time to ponder over those reservations. In a matter of months, the Berlin Programme became out of date in the wake of the collapse of the Berlin Wall in November 1989 (Pautz 2009: 132).

The Austrian SPÖ underwent a similar process of reform. Following the 1983 electoral defeat, the party, now led by Fred Sinowatz, started a process of gradually abandoning Austro-Keynesianism and the progressive ideas of Bruno Kreisky and of slowly adopting a monetarist approach to the economy (Guger 2001: 53–4). In Belgium and the Netherlands, social democrats initially resisted the neoliberal winds that had started to blow in Europe, but that resistance did not contribute to electoral successes (Kitschelt 1994: 2). In the Netherlands the ideological retreat was manifest in the PvdA's cutting of ties with the Industrial Workers' Union. This move led to a decline in the party's membership which impacted its electoral performance (Keman 2023: 151).

In Denmark, the social democrats spent a decade in opposition following several failed attempts to solve the economic crisis, and were punished by voters at the 1984 election. After that defeat, the Danish Social Democrats started an incremental revisionist process similar to Sweden's "Third Way", but it was only in the 1990s that they adopted a more centrist approach (Green-Pedersen & van Kersbergen 2002). That centrist approach still involved a commitment to full employment, but it also included changes to pensions policy and the adoption of active labour market policies.

The different types of reforms experienced by European social democratic parties in a period shaped by the acceleration of globalization and the deepening of the project of European integration was consequential. The different experiences meant that these parties disagreed not only about how to pursue social democracy but they also clashed about the direction of the project of European integration. The lack of unity in the European social democratic family strengthened the case of liberal and conservative governments. Without a strong social democratic opposition, they could develop a European project with a strong neoliberal flavour.

The electoral misfortunes of social democratic parties as well as the programmatic reforms they adopted later resulted from three key factors: (1) demographic changes to the core electorate of social democratic parties; (2) the intensification of economic globalization and in particular the neoliberal turn in the process of European integration; (3) a crisis of ideas driven by the triumph of neoliberalism and the collapse of communism in the Soviet Union and in eastern, central and Baltic Europe.

A changing electorate

The crisis of European social democracy was first manifest in the successive electoral defeats suffered by social democratic parties in the late 1970s and early 1980s. Those defeats reflected wider demographic changes in society, namely the shrinking of the industrial working class which resulted from the process of deindustrialization. The shift to post-industrial economies that took place in the late 1960s and 1970s resulted in the growth of private non-industrial employment (Pontusson 1995: 496; Benedetto *et al.* 2020: 938) and in the significant reduction of the unionized working class.

The shrinking in size of the working class severely impacted the electoral fortunes of social democratic parties. This being said, the impact of these changes should not be exaggerated. After all, the working class never constituted the majority in any European country and was rarely the only electorate of social democratic parties (Przeworski & Sprague 1986: 3). The electoral coalitions of social democratic parties always included agrarian workers (in Sweden, Denmark and France), public sector workers and liberal professionals (Przeworski 1993: 102–3).

In addition, the impact of these economic and demographic changes varied across the different social democratic parties. In countries such as Britain the decline in the industrial working class resulting from deindustrialization dealt a severe blow to the Labour Party which historically relied heavily on the support of this group of voters. Similarly, in Denmark the Social Democrats lost roughly 10 per cent of their working-class voters in the period 1973–87. But in Sweden, the unionized working class continued to make up more than 50 per cent of the SAP's electoral base. Similarly, in Germany the SPD was able to keep the support of working-class voters at a relatively stable level between 1969 and 1987 (Moschonas 1998). In countries such as Portugal and France, the socialist parties had weaker institutional links to trade unions and faced competition from strong communist parties, and therefore relied on a more diverse, although more volatile, electoral coalition of voters.

What is clear is that from the 1980s and in response to these demographic changes, social democratic parties sought to diversify their electoral coalitions with programmes and campaigns that diluted their class nature. But this strategy was not risk-free. Social democratic parties faced difficult electoral trade-offs (Bandau 2022: 494), although there is no consensus about their shape and impact. For instance, Przeworski and Sprague argued that workers were "less likely to vote socialist when parties accumulate electoral support from other groups" (1986: 88). They also argued that the impact depended on factors such as the presence of strong communist parties in the party system. Hence, when social democratic parties competed with strong communist parties, their catch-all strategies implied "steep trade-offs". As they illustrated, for each middle-class voter the French socialists recruited, 9.3 working-class votes were lost (Przeworski & Sprague 1986: 71). But when trade unions had the specific role of organizing voters as a class, social democratic parties could afford to pursue catch-all strategies at a relatively low cost to their support among workers (Przeworski & Sprague 1986: 79).

Kitschelt challenged this thesis. For him voting preferences are less determined by social class than Przeworski and Sprague assumed. As he explained, "it is not class in the Marxian sense but a variety of market and organizational experiences, as well as experiences in the reproductive sphere of social relations, that shape political consciousness" (Kitschelt 1993: 299). Crucially, that political consciousness was expressed not only in the capitalist–socialist scale but also along a libertarian–authoritarian axis (Kitschelt 1994: 45). What this meant was that the support of the working class was no longer important enough for social democratic parties to forsake a strategy that was "more libertarian, yet more moderate on distributive economic issues" (Kitschelt 1994: 301). Merkel concurred but he framed the dilemma slightly differently. Instead of emphasizing the market and societal factors that shaped the political consciousness of voters, he specifically identified the new postmaterialist demands and the decline of egalitarian values among considerable segments of the middle classes as the factors that "created a strategic dilemma" for social democratic parties (Merkel 1989: 6).

It turns out that most European social democratic parties followed the electoral strategy suggested by Kitschelt, which involved the dilution of egalitarian commitments and the focus on postmaterial values.

The neoliberal turn in European integration

The second factor that drove the transformation of social democracy was the impact of globalization on the state's ability to decide its economic policies and in particular the neoliberal turn[3] in the project of European integration. The Treaty of Rome of 1957 envisaged the creation of a European single market where competition law would be enforced by a powerful European Court of Justice at some undefined time in the future, but changes to the division of labour in the global economy in the 1980s rendered that goal more urgent. Thus, the EU started a neo-liberal/ordoliberal turn which privileged a small and fiscally responsible state in the economic sphere and implied welfare retrenchment, flexible labour markets, the weakening of trade unions (which led to a rise in insecure work and a decline in wages) and robust competition rules that prevented state aid to national industries in crisis.

This neoliberal turn – which was expressed in the Single European Act of 1985, the single market and the Maastricht Treaty of 1992 that transformed the EC into the EU and announced the first steps of the European Monetary Union – prioritized market values over a "social Europe".[4] The policies and rules associated with these different projects, and in particular the new powers of European institutions, constrained the ability of states to protect (let alone develop) their welfare states, to promote full employment and workers' rights and to shield public services from semi-privatization, or market-driven reforms, and economic deregulation. Above all, the convergence criteria signed in the 1992 Maastricht Treaty sealed the ordoliberal direction of the single currency (Blyth 2013: 141).[5]

Crucially, these changes tied the hands of future social democratic governments. As Moschonas explained, the strengthening of the EU and its institutions "functioned as a double institutional trap for the future: first, by gridlocking the neo-liberal logic at the EU level and, second, by the weakening of national institutions and the associated difficulty in countering neo-liberal logic at the national level" (2009: 169). In addition, the fragmentation of European governance over several layers of transnational, national and local levels, acted as a hindrance to the initiatives of social democratic governments (Moschonas 2009: 173). These changes were highly consequential for European social democracy. The development of a social democratic European project would now require a radical transformation of the entire European policymaking architecture (Lordon 2015).

Europe's social democratic parties were aware of these challenges. In 1990, at the European Council summit in Madrid, social democratic leaders recognized that the internationalization of the economy hindered the ability of governments to respond to new problems at a national level. In subsequent initiatives and gatherings, the Party of European Socialists (PES) and the Socialist International tried to counter the neoliberal turn with an emphasis on "social Europe" and myriad proposals aimed at promoting full employment and social rights.

But this effort was too little and too late. As noted by Ladrech (1999) and Andry (2022), social democratic parties are partly responsible for the EU's neoliberal turn, as they accepted its logic, although it is equally true that this acceptance was not born out of conviction for most of them. The social democratic acceptance of the EU's neoliberal turn was the result of an unfavourable balance of powers in the EU (now dominated by centre-right governments) which in turn led to the acceptance of the idea that in the new globalized world the state no longer had the capacity to reform capitalism.

Feeling powerless, several social democratic parties approved many of these policies. In some cases, they had also opened the way for the neoliberal turn in the EU. In the 1970s, the British Labour government led by James Callaghan declared the end of Keynesian economics and the German SPD government led by Helmut Schmidt had a key role in paving the way to that neoliberal turn. Similarly, the decision of François Mitterrand to abandon his radical social democratic agenda and deploy an austerity turn was extremely consequential for other European social democrats. The European project that countries such as Greece, Spain and Portugal, and later Austria, Finland and Sweden, joined (in 1995) was markedly different from the project launched in the 1950s.

Their hope was to develop a vague "social Europe" alongside the monetary union, which would mitigate the effects of some of the neoliberal reforms. Others, such as the Danish Social Democrats, offered some resistance to the neoliberal logic by negotiating opt-outs from the European Monetary Union (Sweden followed the same path when it joined the EU in 1995). In their view, the governance rules of the single currency were a threat to their welfare states. Eventually, social democrats lost this battle and ended up capitulating to the logic that prioritized the European project over social democratic goals.

By the late 1990s, the neoliberal turn of the EU was not only a reality but also became the guiding line of EU governance. From then on, even the initiatives aimed at protecting social and economic rights, such as the European Social Chapter of the Maastricht Treaty, the "social" dispositions of the Treaty of Amsterdam, the 2000 Lisbon Agenda and the Stability and Growth Pact of 1997 (which underwent several revisions since then), privileged a Europe of markets. In other words, the EU did not adopt the version of "social Europe" (discussed in Chapter 2) which was promoted in the 1970s by social democratic parties and European commissioners and did not propose to extend workers' rights in the workplace.

The institutionalization of the EU's neoliberal turn had far-reaching consequences for European social democracy: it imposed severe constraints on the ability of social democratic governments to govern in a social democratic way, as it narrowed the range of policy initiatives they could develop and limited the ambition of their programmes. Interestingly, the neoliberal turn of the EU also resulted in greater policy and ideological convergence across Europe, and that in turn resulted in a greater uniformity of social democratic practices.

An identity crisis

In addition to the demographic changes to the electoral coalitions of social democratic parties, the impact of globalization, the EU's neoliberal turn and the global triumph of neoliberalism, the collapse of communism in the Soviet Union and eastern and central Europe in the period 1989–91 contributed to the identity crisis of European social democracy. It must be said that European social democracy had been staunchly anti-communist since the establishment of the Third International by Lenin in 1919. However, while communist regimes existed, social democratic parties had incentives to maintain a modicum of loyalty to their socialist identities.

The collapse of communism removed that incentive and enabled the parties of the centre-right to claim that they had "won" the ideological war and that there were no alternatives to the market. In the process they reinforced the supremacy of neoliberal values in powerful political circles. Confronted with TINA (There Is No Alternative), European social democrats concluded that the formula "Keynesianism and welfare state" was past its sell-by date. The problem was that social democrats had no alternatives of their own to propose. As a result, they ended up following the neoliberal path, although not wholeheartedly.

This realization transformed the type of social democracy on offer in western Europe, but it also shaped the social democracy that was emerging in eastern, central and Baltic Europe. The new social democratic parties that were formed following the collapse of communist regimes were keen to dissociate themselves from any vestiges of Marxism and Soviet communism. In programmatic terms this meant that the social democratic parties of former communist countries supported and enacted programmes of privatizations, economic liberalization and retrenchment of the welfare state (Tavits & Letki 2009), although they tended to be "less libertarian and more traditional" on social and cultural values than western European social democratic parties (Holmes & Lightfoot 2011: 47). Slovakia's Direction – Social Democracy, which formed an alliance with a far-right party, is an example of that tendency (Holmes & Lightfoot 2011: 43).

The neoliberalization of the new social democratic parties was partly forced by the logic of the transitions to democracy and to market economies and by the process of joining the EU. Typically, in post-communist Europe social democrats started to win elections in the mid-1990s but only after the first elected governments had disappointed voters by introducing drastic cuts to welfare programmes, privatizing most industries and liberalizing the economy. Disillusioned voters expected the new social democratic parties to govern with a stronger "left-wing" identity. That expectation resulted in the victory of social democratic parties in Poland (1993), Hungary (1994) and Czechia (1998) (Vachudova 2013: 47).

But once in office, social democratic parties implemented neoliberal policies (Ágh 2004: 3), namely the privatization of industries, the liberalization of labour markets and the introduction of cuts to social and welfare spending. These parties felt that they had to introduce neoliberal economic reforms to demonstrate to voters and to the world outside their dissociation from Soviet communism and their ability to manage a liberal democracy and market economy (Tavits & Letki 2009: 555).

In Poland, the Democratic Left Alliance (SLD), a party that emerged from the old communist party but which adopted a neoliberal identity, won the elections and formed a coalition with the agrarian Polish People's Party. The SLD government continued the neoliberal reforms of its predecessors which involved cuts to welfare spending, liberalization and privatization programmes, which in turn led to a substantial rise in unemployment (Zubek 1994: 813–14).

In Hungary, there were several parties that claimed a social democratic identity. Following the transition to democracy, the Social Democratic Party (MSzP) made up of former communists maintained an allegiance to vague Marxist traditions and to democratic socialism and European welfare values (Racz 1993: 648). But by the 1990s the MSzP was determined to show that it was committed to democracy and the market economy (Racz 1993: 660–1). In 1994 the MSzP became the governing party and implemented "forceful and far-reaching reforms that the preceding right-wing government had failed to introduce" (Tavits & Letki 2009: 559). Similarly, in Czechia the Social Democratic Party led a coalition government in 1998 with the main centre-right party which spearheaded a privatization programme.

The Baltic states followed a similar path despite their different points of origins. The Lithuanian Democratic Labour Party and Estonia's Social Democratic Party (The Moderates until 2003) endorsed a neoliberal programme that involved liberalization, privatizations and cuts to the welfare state. The conversion to market values was so strong in Estonia that party leaders were reluctant to adopt the name Social Democratic Party because of its negative connotations (Tavits & Letki 2009: 565–6), while in Latvia the social democratic party was (and remains) a minor player in the country's politics.

In Bulgaria, the post-communist left followed a different path, at least for a while. The Bulgarian Socialist Party (formerly a communist party) maintained a leftist identity and was reluctant to start economic reforms, but by 1997 this stance was untenable given the deterioration of economic circumstances and Bulgaria's hopes to join the EU. Thus, in that year, the Bulgarian Socialist Party implemented a range of reforms that aimed to liberalize and reorient the Bulgarian economy to the free market standards demanded by the EU. To that end, the socialist government introduced cuts to welfare benefits and pensions and introduced a flat tax. The Romanian Social Democratic Party followed a similar trajectory: initially it resisted economic reforms but eventually, in the early 2000s, it adopted neoliberal policies (Tavits & Letki 2009: 566).

In short, the new variant of social democracy that emerged in eastern, central and Baltic Europe was distinct from the other varieties of European social democracy in the sense that it was not shaped by the weight of 100 years of doctrinal debates and adaptation to new political and economic circumstances. For these reasons it was ready to nimbly adopt and adapt the dominant set of values and programmes to which all varieties of social democracy converged in the 1990s. As we saw, this choice was as much the result of deliberate choices as it was of external constraints. Joining the EU narrowed the range of possibilities for social democratic governments not only in eastern, central and Baltic Europe but, also, across the continent.

Social democratic convergence

As explained earlier in the chapter, the first parties to succumb to the logic of neoliberal convergence were the French socialists and the parties of the new democracies in southern Europe, that is, parties without strong institutional links to trade unions and with relatively incipient activist bases. These parties adopted a "modernization" approach that meant social democratic values had to be sacrificed in the name of the European project.

In the case of Italy, the transformation was striking. The modernized and neo-revisionist PSI, which had been in government throughout the 1980s, imploded in the early 1990s following the anti-corruption investigation "*mani pulite*" (clean hands). As the PSI collapsed, the PCI underwent its own transformation in the period 1989–91, which culminated in the celebration of the collapse of communism in eastern and central Europe, the death of Eurocommunism and the emergence of the Democratic Party of the Left (PDS) under the leadership of Achille Occhetto. In a single sweep, the PDS now claimed to be a democratic socialist party, which joined the Socialist International and the PES. The move proved to be astute: the PDS was the second most popular party at the 1992 elections.

The party participated in the 1997 elections under a loose umbrella organization of 12 left-wing parties and movements of the left called

L'Ulivo. Capitalizing on the unpopularity of the socialists, L'Ulivo won those elections with 43.7 per cent of the vote. This was a historic moment as the ex-Communist left entered the Italian government for the first time since 1947. However, L'Ulivo did not stay in power for long. Romano Prodi, who had fronted the 1997 election, lost a confidence vote after the government's communist allies withdrew support for his deficit-reducing budget and was replaced by the former communist Massimo D'Alema in 1998.

In Britain, the Labour Party sought to understand the causes of its four consecutive electoral defeats since 1979 and accelerated its modernization process when Tony Blair was elected party leader in 1994. Tellingly, Labour did not look much to Europe as a source of inspiration. As the Labour strategist Philip Gould put it, "there was little evidence of fresh thinking, new ideas or a drive to modernise" in European sister parties (1998: 180). Despite Gould's misgivings, New Labour's flagship job-creation programme New Deal was inspired by Danish and Dutch active labour market policies.

By the time Blair was elected leader the most difficult and controversial and programmatic reforms had been implemented by his predecessors. However, the New Labour leader was determined to go further than Neil Kinnock and John Smith in the party's modernization drive. Driving this process was Blair's understanding of the world in the 1990s. He argued that globalization was "the driving force of economic change" which social democrats should accept. For Blair the task for social democratic governments was to equip citizens, through new investments in education and new active labour market policies, to compete in the new economy while maintaining stable macroeconomic policies, adopting transparent financial systems, promoting competition and investment in economic infrastructure and accepting "the disciplines of the international economy" (Blair 1996).

Blair's modernization drive was also motivated by the desire to win the following elections. Given the changes to the composition of Labour's electoral coalition, Blair was aware that winning required widening the party's electoral base. But to achieve that goal, Labour had to show British voters that it had radically changed. It is in this context that Blair proposed to change the totemic Clause Four from the party's constitution, which had committed Labour to the principle of collective ownership of the means of production.

This proposal was seen as "heretical" by party members, but for the modernizers the move was about putting an end to the confusion between the means and ends of social democracy (Wright 1997: 26). Eventually, the modernizers won the debate and Clause Four was reformulated along communitarian lines.[6] Blair also started to refer to the party as New Labour, as a tactic to persuade voters that the party had changed and was proposing a fresh agenda. This agenda offered a "Third Way" between neoliberalism and "old" social democracy and as an approach that adapted Labour's traditional goals to the challenges posed by the new globalized world. Blair's reformist drive paid off and Labour won a landslide victory at the 1997 general election.

Germany's SPD experienced a similar neo-revisionist process. In 1992, German social democrats tried to come to terms with the new political, economic and geopolitical realities they faced by endorsing a party programme which combined an allegiance to ordoliberal fiscal responsibility and a commitment to invest in public services and in training programmes for the unemployed (Pautz 2009: 133). But the party remained divided. There was an influential left-wing faction, led by Oskar Lafontaine, that wanted to retain the party's social democratic identity, and a powerful right-wing faction, led by Gerhard Schröder, that insisted on adapting the party to the forces of globalization.

By the time of the 1998 election, the SPD's adaptation to the neoliberal orthodoxy was practically complete. In particular, the party agreed that any attempt to regulate markets would be accompanied by capital flight, devaluation, inflation and recession (Schmidt 2016: 133). Under the impulse of Schröder, who was inspired by Blair's Third Way, the SPD fought the 1998 elections as the party of the *Neue Mitte* (the new centre) (Pautz 2009: 134).

Interestingly, the concept of *Neue Mitte* was ambiguous. Although it was clearly inspired by Blair's Third Way, the term *Neue Mitte* was, as recalled by Busch and Manow (2001: 180), used by Willy Brandt in the early 1970s and was a direct reference to the socialist traditions of the revolutions of 1848. In this light, it is perhaps not surprising that the 1998 programme was a somewhat incoherent mix of neo-revisionism and traditional social democracy. The programme used the language of full employment and stakeholder society, and it promised to reverse the cuts to unemployment benefits and sick pay introduced by the centre-right coalition government, but it defended a leaner and more efficient state committed to low inflation (Pautz 2009: 135).

The Dutch followed a similar modernizing path, although it is worth remembering that the PvdA had metamorphosed from a working-class into a catch-all party soon after the Second World War. By the 1990s, the party was perfectly at ease in the ideology-light world of coalition politics. Indeed, the PvdA leader and Dutch Prime Minister Wim Kok argued that the party "should shake off its ideological feathers" (Kok quoted by Keman 2017: 160).

In Scandinavia, the intensification of globalization and the liberalization of international trade, changes to parties' electoral coalitions and the acceptance that socialism within the nation state was no longer a possibility led to some ideological reckoning within social democratic parties. A visible sign of that reckoning were attitudes to the European project. In the past, social democratic parties in Sweden, Norway and Finland had resisted EU membership in order to protect their social democratic welfare states. But the impact of globalization led Sweden and Finland to seek membership of the EU.

In 1991, Sweden's SAP declared low inflation to be its main priority (and not full employment) and the government of Göran Persson decided to cap public expenditure (Tsarouhas 2009: 116) and join the EU in 1995. However, he remained sceptical about Sweden's participation in the single currency (Vartiainen 2001: 51). By 2001, the SAP had separated the market from capitalism in its economic analysis and reconceptualized the former as a neutral instrument for resource redistribution (Andersson 2016: 122). In Norway, the Labour Party neglected its socialist values and campaigned instead on the themes of individualism and freedom and accepted that the public sector was too large and the state too interfering (Sassoon 1997: 736).

In Denmark, and following more than a decade in opposition, the Social Democrats adopted a manifesto which promised to control public spending, although it kept its commitment to economic democracy (Green-Pedersen & van Kersbergen 2002: 516). It was only in 1993, under the leadership of Poul Nyrup Rasmussen, that the Danish Social Democrats endorsed a neo-revisionist agenda as a way of showing voters that they were responsible managers of the economy (Green-Pedersen & van Kersbergen 2002: 516). The new agenda represented a significant programmatic shift. The reforms to retirement policies and the new focus on active labour market policies represented a departure from the traditional social democratic promotion of generous and universal welfare provision.

Finland's Social Democratic Party (SDP), led by Paavo Lipponen (who defined his approach as liberal), was luckier. In 1995 it obtained its best result since the Second World War thanks in large part to a pro-EU membership approach (Finland joined the EU in 1995) and to the party's programmatic reforms undertaken following the 1991 defeat. At the time, the programmatic reforms were justified on the grounds of the impact of globalization and of the collapse of the Soviet Union in Finland's economy and labour market (Raunio 2010: 194). The change in direction paid off electorally: the social democrats won the election and led a "rainbow coalition" which included the National Coalition, the Left Alliance, the Green League and the Swedish People's Party (Raunio 2010: 190). The programme the party eventually adopted in 1999 focused on core social democratic values and policies such as full employment and the protection of the welfare state alongside the promise to keep budgetary discipline and monetary stability (Raunio 2010: 195) and to reduce labour and social security costs (Fagerholm 2013: 550).

As shown earlier, the pink wave of social democratic-led governments also reached eastern, central and Baltic Europe, albeit on a more modest scale. The social democrats won elections in Czechia (1998) and they were in power in Poland, Hungary and Bulgaria. These parties were elected as voters expressed discontent and disillusion with the transition to a market economy. However, instead of humanizing capitalism, the new social democratic left in eastern and central Europe doubled down on economic liberalization and welfare state retrenchment.

An emerging neo-revisionism

The shrinking of the industrial working class as a group of voters, the emergence of new democracies in eastern, central and Baltic Europe, the acceleration of international free trade and the neoliberal turn of the EU pushed social democratic parties rightwards and towards a neo-liberalized path. From Lisbon to Sofia, from Rome to Stockholm, social democrats embraced market values and consequently endorsed fiscal discipline, diluted their commitment to social and labour rights as an achievable goal and accepted that welfare states had to be reformed and retrenched and public services modernized.[7] They retained a commitment to poverty-reduction strategies and to the principle of redistribution of wealth as well as an attachment to the idea of "social Europe".

The analysis of 19 social democratic party manifestoes by Andreas Fagerholm shows that these parties "moved considerably towards the neoliberal right" in the period 1970–99 (2013: 547–51). This neoliberal trend was "most obvious" within the Luxembourg's Socialist and Workers' Party, Belgium's Socialist Party of Wallonia, the Dutch PvdA, the Socialist Party of Flanders and Austria's SPÖ. There were also "sharp rightward shifts" within Italy's PSI in the 1980s, Britain's Labour Party, the Spanish PSOE and the Finnish SDP in the 1990s, while in parties such as Germany SPD, the Norwegian Labour Party and the Danish Social Democrats there was zigzagging between neoliberal positions and a return to more social democratic positions (Fagerholm 2013: 547–51).

This rightward shift also aimed to build a new electoral coalition which relied mostly on professional and urban workers, the aspirational suburban middle classes and, of course, the remnant of industrial workers, which in some countries still constituted a sizeable group of voters. In organizational terms, social democratic parties loosened their links to trade unions, centralized the process of decision-making in the hands of the leadership and personalized their electoral campaigns around the party leader (Paterson & Sloam 2006: 235). In turn, these party leaders turned to pollsters, focus groups and image consultants who advised them to treat voters as consumers of political programmes, neglected their activist base and consequently became more distanced from their programmatic goals. Activists and members were treated as supporting cheerleaders and useful campaigners, whereas the party leaders and their team were deciding the programme and electoral strategy. In the process, references to the values of social democracy were increasingly absent from party programmes.

The result of these changes was a profound transformation – programmatic, ideological and organizational – of the character of European social democracy (Kitschelt 1994: 2). As Eley noted, "no one talked any longer of abolishing capitalism, of regulating its dysfunctions and excesses, or even modifying its most egregiously destructive social effects" (2002: vii). Those changes were so profound that Sassoon classify them as a new form social democratic "neo-revisionism" (1997: 734–5), while Moschonas defined them as "moderate neoliberalism" (2002: 228) and Nancy Fraser named them as "progressive neoliberalism" (2019). These changes did not amount to the transformation of European social democratic parties into fully fledged neoliberal parties. After all, these parties remained committed to social justice and implemented robust anti-poverty strategies and forms of redistribution of wealth by stealth, but crucially they no longer believed in the power of the state to transform society and accepted neoliberal orthodoxies about the role of the state in the economy. In short, they accepted the primacy of markets over politics (Berman 2006). Tony Blair's claim at the 2005 Labour Party annual conference that wanting to discuss globalization was tantamount to "debate whether autumn should follow summer"[8] was representative of social democrats' uncritical acceptance of globalization. According to this view, there was nothing that could be done about globalization. The only credible response was to reject protectionism, promote competition and free trade and equip citizens with the tools to compete in the new global economy with new investments in education and economic infrastructure and active labour market policies. But, as Dani Rodrik argued, this stance neglects the fact that "globalisation is consciously shaped by the rules that the authorities choose to enact: the groups they privilege, the fields of policy they tackle and those they lay off, and which markets they subject to international competition" (2017). The implication of this is that globalization can be altered to pursue other goals. But that was not the path chosen by the neo-revisionist social democratic parties.

More seriously, the embrace of free market capitalism and the support for the financialization of the economy and all that it entailed trapped social democrats in an economic policy with clear limits. This approach did not contribute to reversing the rise in inequality trends that had been observed since the 1980s. If anything, inequality continued to rise in Europe until 2008 partly as result of regressive tax policies (Fredriksen 2012). Above all, this transformation suggested that social democrats were now resigned to remedial politics (Przeworski 2001). But, as suggested by Patrick Diamond, by resigning themselves to the status quo they forgot "they could still be the agent[s] of change, not simply the inheritor of a pre-existing settlement" (2021: 98).

Beyond left and right

Across Europe, most social democratic parties adopted neo-revisionist programmes on pragmatic grounds. They accepted the governing constraints imposed by trade liberalization and European integration and were not ready to challenge them. But for Britain's Labour Party this process was not only about a pragmatic accommodation to new economic realities. For Blair these reforms reflected an intellectual reassessment of the meaning of social democracy in the age of globalization and which amounted to a new political paradigm that needed to be theorized and internationalized. And that is exactly what he tried to do. Once installed in Downing Street, Blair stimulated an intellectual debate within the international social democratic family which included the United States' Democratic Party led by Bill Clinton (Mudge 2018).

Blair's modernizing agenda was heavily influenced by the New Democrat platform of Clinton, which in turn was inspired by the claim that the "the end of big government is over", by the communitarian ideas of the political philosopher Amitai Etzioni, by the punitive welfare reforms defended by Republicans and paternalistic thinkers such as Lawrence Mead and by the social capital ideas of the American sociologist Robert Putnam and others. This communitarian approach also had the advantage of being compatible with the socialist values of fraternity and cooperation while enabling (through the motto "rights and responsibilities") Labour to dilute its commitments to egalitarian goals.[9] The influence of the New Democrats was also visible in the language deployed by New Labour and other modernizers. For example, the concept of social democracy was often replaced by the words "progressive" and "centre-left" (Mudge 2018: 364).

Anthony Giddens was another key intellectual influence in the debates about social democracy, in particular his analysis of globalization and modernity. In *Beyond Left and Right*, Giddens argued that globalization had led to the emergence of a post-traditional social order, where traditions were still relevant but now "open to interrogation" (1994: 4–5). The implications of this insight for the social democratic left were immense: social democracy could only survive if social democrats were "prepared to revise their pre-existing views more thoroughly" (Giddens 1998, vii). Giddens claimed that Third Way politics should preserve a "core concern with social justice", advocate a mixed economy and adopt the motto "no rights without responsibilities" (1998: 65–6).

Giddens was one of the intellectuals asked by Blair to join the Third Way International circuit, first in the United States and later across Europe and other parts of the world. The moment seemed propitious as 12 out 15 EU member states were governed by social democratic leaders. After setting the terms of the debate with the New Democrats, Blair presented his new gospel in a series of conferences and events around the world which involved figures such as the German Chancellor Gerhard Schröder, the Italian Prime Minister Romano Prodi (replaced at the end of 1999 by Massimo D'Alema), the Swedish Prime Minister Göran Persson, the Dutch Prime Minister Wim Kok, the Polish President Aleksander Kwaśniewski and the Brazilian President Fernando Henrique Cardoso.

In continental Europe, the most enthusiastic endorser of the Third Way was Schröder. So much so that in 1998, Blair and Schröder

Tony Blair, Gerhard Schroeder and Jacques Chirac (*left to right*), 2003, Berlin

Source: Agencja Fotograficzna Caro / Alamy Stock Photo.

co-signed a Fabian Pamphlet where they explained their Third Way/ *Neue Mitte* approach to politics. In this pamphlet, both leaders criticized social democracy for its equation of social justice with equality of outcome and defended free markets. As they put it, "flexible markets are a modern social democratic aim" (Blair & Schröder 1998).

Very quickly neo-revisionist or Third Way ideas dominated debates about the future of social democracy. However, what made these ideas irresistible was the ongoing liberalization of international trade and the neoliberal drive of the EU. The new democracies of eastern, central and Baltic Europe not only did not resist this neoliberal drive but embraced it with enthusiasm. This was particularly true in Poland where the president, the former communist turned social democrat Aleksander Kwaśniewscki, was one of Blair's allies in the Third Way International.

Social democratic governments nonetheless tried to mitigate the negative impact of international trade liberalization and of the neo-liberalization of the EU by insisting on poverty-reduction strategies, investing in public services (especially in education), equipping workers to compete in the globalized economy through active labour market policies and demanding the development of an ill-defined "social Europe". In addition, a variety of social democratic governments introduced new rights to minorities (namely the right to equal marriage to homosexual couples), strengthened legislation on gender equality and committed themselves to tackling climate change. However, and as the new initiatives to promote employment and social inclusion indicated, the Third Way's approach to "social Europe" had neoliberal contours. The 2000 Lisbon Strategy aimed to turn the EU in the most competitive, dynamic, knowledge-based economy in the world and placed the emphasis on economic competitiveness and neglected "social Europe". Instead of commitments to full employment and new social, labour and economic rights, the emphasis was on equipping workers with the skills they needed to compete in the global economy.

The last call for social Europe

While northern, eastern and central European social democrats were quietly seduced by the mood music of the Third Way and *Neue Mitte*, in France, Belgium and southern Europe and on the left of the SPD the reaction was different. It was one thing to accept the limitations that globalization, international capitalism and the EU imposed on social democratic governments; it was quite another to claim that this was the new paradigm for social democracy. For that reason, Blair's efforts to set up a Third Way International were viewed with suspicion by some European social democrats. For some, it looked as if Blair and Clinton were trying to supplant the Socialist International (Mudge 2018).

The strongest resistance to Blair's and Schröder's Third Way came from the PSF led by Lionel Jospin. In 1997, the PSF won the legislative elections with a comfortable plurality and was able to form a coalition government with other parties of the left, including the communists and the greens, and which gained the name of government of the Plural Left. As explained earlier, the French socialists were the second (after the German SPD led by Helmut Schmidt) to sign up to the ordoliberal orthodoxy, but in the late 1990s they believed there was sufficient fiscal space to pursue broadly Keynesian economic policies, which included the flagship policy to reduce the working week to 35 hours (Clift 2009: 76). In the European sphere, Jospin was ready to support the launch of the monetary union along ordoliberal lines, but on the condition that a "social Europe" agenda was to pursued by "European economic government, representing the people, charged with co-ordinating economic policies" and founded on a solidarity and growth pact (Clift 2009: 81).

The Belgian social democrats were equally sceptical of Third Way politics. Frank Vandenbroucke, then leader of the Flemish Socialists and Belgium vice-prime minister, argued that the intellectual framework of the Third Way was "not only wrong", but it also hampered New Labour's capacity "to engage thoroughly in key debates within European social democracy, such as the management of the euro, the future of collective bargaining, the future of budgetary politics, the future of the European model tout court". He also accused those neo-revisionist social democrats of reviewing "if not their deepest values, at least their standards of justice" (Vandenbroucke 2001: 166–8).

In Spain the PSOE had similar instincts, but as a party that had lost the 1996 elections following corruption scandals, the Spanish socialists had little influence in European debates until they won the 2004 legislative elections (Kennedy 2009: 99). The Portuguese Socialist Party (PS), in power since 1995, were able to develop a halfway position between the Third Way and the ideas of "social Europe", simultaneously implementing a Basic Income for Social Inclusion and an ambitious privatization programme and signing up to the monetary union. The socialist leader António Guterres was a moderate catholic socialist who understood that for a small, poor country such as Portugal, meeting the requirements of EU membership took priority over social democratic values. But if he accepted the rigour imposed by the Maastricht convergence criteria, he insisted, like Jospin, in the development of a "social Europe". In Greece, PASOK held an ambivalent line about European integration. On the one hand, the party believed that the euro's convergence criteria would allow a PASOK government to introduce reforms that would address structural problems in the Greek economy, but on the other hand, it hoped for the emergence of a "social Europe" (Dimitrakopoulos & Passas 2011: 136–8).

The unravelling of the Third Way

These changes were hugely significant for European social democracy. In the process of embracing the market and accepting globalization as a divine force about which nothing could be done, social democracy abandoned its historical critique of capitalism and accepted the subordination of politics to market discipline. Crucially, this neo-revisionism ended up biting the social democrats who were in government at the beginning of the new century. Within months of putting the new euro notes and coins into circulation, member states started to struggle to comply with the eurozone governance rules. Famously, Germany was the first European country to break the deficit rules of the Maastricht convergence criteria, but France and Portugal quickly followed suit.

The birthing pains of the single currency, and the deteriorating economic conditions across the world in the early 2000s, led to the unravelling of the Third Way wave. The broad coalition of voters that supported social democratic parties in the 1990s started to abandon them (Benedetto *et al.* 2020: 939). One by one, social democratic governments begun to collapse like domino pieces. Massimo D'Alema was the first one to go in 1999 following a defeat in regional elections and difficulties in managing the coalition government. The Portuguese prime minister and leader of the Socialist International, António Gutteres, resigned in 2001 following poor results at the local elections, paving the way for early legislative elections and a centre-right government. The socialists were back in power in 2005, winning a surprising first landslide victory in the history of the party. However, they were not able to implement social democratic policies as they had to comply with the deficit requirements of the euro. In France, the government of the Plural Left did not last much longer. Jospin, who had decided to run for the French presidency, was eliminated in the first round of the 2002 elections. A couple of months later, the Socialist Party suffered a resounding defeat at the legislative elections. In Greece, PASOK lost its hold on power (which it had held since 1980) in the elections of 2004.

In northern Europe, social democratic parties also started to lose elections but for different reasons. Instead of economic woes caused by the constraints of the monetary union (only Finland and the Netherlands were part of the single currency), in northern Europe social democrats were being challenged by the rise in salience of popular concerns with immigration and multicultural values and resistance to higher welfare spending. In Denmark, the Rasmussen government was defeated in the 2001 elections, mostly because of the rise in popularity of an anti-immigration party, and remained in opposition for a decade.

In 2002, the Dutch PvdA lost the elections because of the rise in popularity of the anti-immigration populist Pim Fortuyn. In 2003, it was the turn of the Finnish SDP to lose popularity, although it still managed to join the coalition government led by the centre-right Centre Party. In Sweden, the SAP obtained its lowest share of the vote since 1911, attracting only 34.99 per cent of the vote and losing votes to the radical right party Sweden Democrats at the 2006 elections. The party remained in opposition until 2014.

In eastern and central Europe, social democrats suffered substantial losses at exactly the time when these countries joined the EU. In Poland, the SLD was reduced to 11.3 per cent share of the vote at the 2005 legislative elections following the introduction of the tax rises and public-spending cuts required to join the EU. In Hungary, following several rounds of spending cuts and corruption scandals, the MSzP lost the 2010 elections, giving way to a government led by the populist party Fidesz (Berman & Snegovaya 2019: 12–13). In both countries, social democrats have remained in opposition ever since.

Those who remained in power introduced reforms that were later rejected by voters. In Germany, the SPD led by Gerhard Schröder lost substantial support following the introduction of the Agenda 2010 labour market reforms. The purpose of these reforms was to consolidate a broader electoral coalition which included former supporters of the Christian Democrats (Camerra-Rowe 2004: 4) who supported cuts to unemployment benefits, as well as a rise of the age of retirement and the liberalization of the labour market (Camerra-Rowe 2004: 1). However, Agenda 2010 was not a successful electoral strategy. In 2005 Schröder lost a confidence vote and was forced to call early elections which the SPD lost. Bitterness and above all ideological differences resulted in the defection of a group of party members led by Oskar Lafontaine who founded the party Die Linke in 2007. The party's divisions and the election defeat did not deter the SPD from pursuing its neoliberalization process. The Hamburg Programme adopted in 2007 defended supply-side economics and politics, and accepted inequalities and globalization, although it also argued that capitalism had to be regulated for the common good (Pautz 2009: 139–41).

In crisis, again

The collapse of the Third Way wave meant that the third act of European social democracy finished as it started: in an existential crisis. In the early 2000s social democratic parties were again in retreat across the continent. The new social democratic revisionism, which sought to address the challenges posed by globalization, the neoliberal turn of the EU and the new geopolitical reality of the continent, as well as the demographic changes to the social democratic electoral coalition, resulted in spectacular short-term electoral gains – 12 governments in Europe led by social democrats in the late 1990s – but in long-term losses.

Unlike other phases of social democratic transformation, the third act of social democracy was mostly the result of incremental changes, namely of processes of conversion and displacement (Streeck & Thelen 2010: 19–29), but which resulted in a dramatic transformation of social democracy. While the belief that nothing could be done about globalization led social democratic parties to dilute commitments to equality and to a tamed form of capitalism, the EU's neoliberal turn consolidated a transformation where, as Przeworski suggested, "something that used to be called 'socialism'" had been abandoned (2001: 312). If in the post-war period the embrace of a transformed and regulated form of capitalism was not an obstacle to social democratic goals, the acceptance of the primacy of markets over politics implied a substantial revision of the goals and values of social democracy. The acceptance of neoliberalism and turbo-charged globalization ruled out the regulation of capitalism that could have prevented or at least mitigated the effects of cycles of "boom and bust" and contributed to the rise of inequalities. As Escalona and Vieira explained, the hallmarks of this type of capitalism were "unstable growth rates, increasing inequalities and an ever-increasing number of speculative bubbles" (2016: 22).

When the economy turned for the worst – as it did in the early 2000s in yet another crisis of capitalism – social democratic governments lost their ability to invest the proceeds of economic growth in public services and to support the most vulnerable. Worse, the constraints imposed by European integration meant that Keynesian responses to the crisis were out of the question. The culmination of this trend was the global financial crisis of 2007–8, which showed beyond reasonable doubt that the social democratic neo-revisionism of the 1990s was not a strategy that guaranteed the survival of social democracy in the Europe of the twenty-first century.

4

Social democracy in a fragmented world

The Third Way wave left European social democracy woefully ill-prepared for the political, economic and social turbulence of the first decades of the twenty-first century. When the global financial crisis of 2007–8 hit Europe, social democrats, who had spent the previous decade praising the dynamism of free markets and accepting light-touch regulation of the financial industry, did not know how to respond to it. However, this crisis was just the firing shot for over a decade of multiple, different and disorientating crises. Following the global financial crisis, Europe was hit by the eurozone crisis of 2010, the refugee crisis of 2015, the rise of the populist and radical right, Brexit, democratic backsliding in eastern and central Europe, the climate emergency, a pandemic, a cost-of-living crisis, an energy crisis and a new war on the European continent. The dizzying speed at which each crisis was followed by another confounded policy-makers.

For social democrats this sense of disorientation was compounded by the loss of an ideological compass in the 1990s which could have offered some guidance on how to respond to these multiple challenges. The uncritical embrace of global capitalism, and in particular of the light-touch approach to financial regulation, which paved way to the global financial crisis left social democratic parties without an economic policy of their own (Manwaring & Kennedy 2018: 180). For these reasons, the crises of the first decades of the twenty-first century posed an existential challenge to European social democracy.

This chapter charts the travails of European social democrats since the global financial crisis of 2007–8. When the crisis started, some believed that the big crisis of capitalism had created a "social democratic moment", that is, it had created a window of opportunity to revive social democracy (Bayley *et al.* 2016: 2). But for a variety of reasons, the elusive social democratic moment metamorphosed into an age of austerity and highly polarized politics which crucially did not insulate Europe from other crises. The chapter explains how this period was marked by the eclipse of electoral social democracy, which partly resulted from new changes to the electoral coalition of social democratic parties. With rare exceptions, social democrats were out of office, and when they were in power, they were too weak and isolated to develop social democratic responses to the multiple challenges they faced (Ryner 2016).

The chapter argues that the fourth act of social democracy is still being written. As it stands the future is uncertain. Social democrats can continue to muddle through with the technocratic, incremental and remedial responses to the challenges they face, or they can engage with the many ideas that have been suggested by left-wing intellectuals and activists and choose a bolder path that could lead to a renewal of the social democratic creed.

From social democratic moment to austerity turn

The global financial crisis caught European policy-makers by surprise. The crisis started with the bursting of the housing bubble in the United States in 2007 but it soon spread to the rest of the global financial system (Gamble 2009: 19). In the United States, banks that had been the backbone of the American housing market were bailed out by the US Treasury. In Britain, the Treasury intervened to stop a bank run in the commercial bank Northern Rock in 2007 and ended up bailing out five commercial banks. Across Europe, policy-makers believed that the European economies were "insulated" from "irresponsible" Anglo-Saxon capitalism, but very soon this assessment proved to be complacent (Gamble 2009: 125). The collapse of the investment bank Lehman Brothers in September 2008 sent a shock wave throughout the world. In the vivid words of Adam Tooze, its impact was "felt on factory floors and in dockyards, financial markets and commodity exchanges around the world" (2018: 1).

By then it was clear that this was not a mere recession. It was a full-blown crisis of capitalism of the type dreamed by socialists in the late nineteenth century but unimagined by the defenders and architects of financialized capitalism. This much was admitted by the former president of the Federal Reserve, Alan Greenspan, when he told the

American Congress that the "whole intellectual edifice ... collapsed" (Greenspan quoted by Goes 2016: 2). Greenspan was not the only one to be confused. In the immediate months that followed the collapse of Lehman Brothers, the *Financial Times* undertook the task of explaining to its perplexed readership of bankers, businesspeople and politicians the significance of this crisis of capitalism. Policy-makers of all political persuasions struggled to understand the causes of the crisis and to find solutions to it. However, social democrats and centre-left politicians felt that this crisis could open the way to a social democratic moment.

The initial response to the global financial crisis seemed to suggest that a new social democratic moment was within its grasp, as the power of the state was used to save capitalism from itself. Under the stewardship of the then British Prime Minister Gordon Brown, the G20 countries met in 2009 and agreed to spend millions of pounds, euros and dollars bailing out and nationalizing failing banks and taking the necessary measures to ensure that the global financial system could continue to operate. The approval of the package was not uncontroversial. The German finance minister, who was at the time the leader of the German SPD, Peer Steinbrück, called this approach adopted at the G20 and EU and G7 summits in 2008 an example of "crass Keynesianism" (Steinbrück quoted by Roder 2019: 178).

Steinbrück's words were ominous. It turns out that bailing out the banks left European governments with high levels of public debt. The ordoliberal architecture of the eurozone did not accept such a state of affairs. Therefore, in Europe, the 12 months of Keynesianism were followed by harsh doses of austerity politics which had the effect of deepening the crisis (Blyth 2013: 56). In many cases, those austerity measures were introduced by social democratic governments.

Even countries who were outside the eurozone succumbed to the austerity logic. In Denmark, the government imposed harsh public-spending cuts which were continued by the social democratic executive following the 2011 elections. In Britain, the Labour government started to cut public spending and raise taxes to the highest income earners. In the eurozone, the ordoliberal rules of the monetary union dictated round after round of public-spending cuts as the appropriate recipe to cut the public deficits that had been created by the public bail-outs of private banks. However, the tightening of the public belt did not result in balanced budgets. In the EU, every country apart from Poland registered negative growth around that time. In Latvia, Hungary and Romania the economic situation was so dire that the EU provided them with emergency financial assistance (Holmes & Roder 2019: 5).

By 2010, the global financial crisis was not only far from over, it had metamorphosed into a eurozone crisis. In October 2009, the Greek prime minister, George Papandreou, revealed that the official Greek public debt and deficit figures had been manipulated. It turns out that Greece's public deficit stood at 15.4 per cent of gross domestic product (GDP) and public debt amounted to 129 per cent of GDP (Sotiropoulos 2016: 202). This revelation set in motion a cycle of events that threatened the solvency of Greece. The PASOK leader and Prime Minister Papandreou's candid admission provoked a dramatic rise in Greece's borrowing costs, which in turn led the credit rating agencies to downgrade Greek sovereign debt to junk status, which in turn contributed to even higher borrowing costs, which by now the Greek government had no capacity to meet.

The rational solution to the crisis was to restructure Greek public debt. But agreeing to it took time as there was too much at stake. The risk of contagion was real. Above all, the eurozone did not have the financial capacity to help defaulting member states stabilize their economies. Under the rules of the Maastricht Treaty, mutual bailouts were banned. Northern European countries were also concerned that debt restructuring could create perverse incentives which could encourage other governments to "live beyond their means". While European leaders debated moral hazard issues, Greece had very few options. As a member of the eurozone the Greek government could not recur to the traditional instruments – such as currency devaluations – to tackle public debt.

Following weeks of hesitations and vicious negotiations, in May 2010 the troika of the European Commission, the European Central Bank and the International Monetary Fund agreed a Memorandum of Understanding which provided Greece with a conditional loan of €110 billion. In exchange for this loan, the Greek government was required to implement eye-watering public-spending cuts, tax rises worth €30 billion and structural reforms to the labour market, as well as to privatize several economic assets and raise the retirement age. Needless to say, the terms of the agreement with the troika plunged Greece into a deep economic recession which eventually resulted in the award of two more bailouts in 2012 and in 2015.

It turned out that this bailout was not a viable solution to either the Greek debt crisis or the eurozone crisis, as it soon spread to other vulnerable economies in the eurozone. By the December of 2010, it was the turn of Ireland to apply for a bailout, and by March 2011 it was the turn of the Portuguese government to approach the troika with a similar request. As in the Greek case, the bailouts to Ireland and Portugal had heavy strings attached. They too had to implement structural reforms which included privatizations and cuts to pensions, public sector pay and welfare spending.

Judging the bailouts and the austerity measures as being insufficient to tackle the crisis, European leaders proceeded to introduce a range of reforms to the governance of the eurozone. The Treaty on Stability, Coordination and the Governance, the adoption of the European Semester and the 6-Pack agreement which introduced the punitive measure euphemistically called the Excessive Deficit Procedure, whereby member states can be fined for breaching the deficit targets agreed with the EU, provided important financial protection to eurozone member states but at the cost of permanent austerity (Streeck 2014: 91).

This approach to the crisis reflected conflicting visions about the purpose and design of the monetary union, inflicted unnecessary economic and social pain and contributed to the polarization of European politics. The main cause of this drama was the misdiagnosis of the crisis (Blyth 2013: 52). If the Greek economy was insolvent in 2009, that was not the case for other European countries. The main causes of the eurozone crisis were excessive financialization of European economies and an incomplete and ill-designed monetary union which treated all members equally and enabled the weaker states to borrow at the same rates as the stronger ones. The monetary union also had a negative impact on the economic competitiveness of those weaker economies, which, thanks to the single currency, were exporting their goods at much higher prices. Moreover, the monetary union also deprived member states of the policy instruments normally deployed at the time of recessions. They could neither devalue their currency nor borrow to stimulate the economy. They simply had to comply with the eurozone governance rules. The result of the shortcomings of the monetary union was greater economic divergence between European economies. According to Mark Blyth, the only "convergence of sorts" it produced was that "everyone except Germany started to run deficits" (Blyth 2013: 79).

The misdiagnosis of the eurozone crisis also led to the wrong pre-scription. Austerity policies led to a deep economic recession, expressed in record levels of unemployment in the European southern periphery, and almost a decade of economic stagnation across the European continent. The management of the eurozone crisis also led to the temporary suspension of democracy. In Greece and Italy, the EU favoured the appointment of technocrats as prime ministers for short periods of time, a decision which contributed to political instability in these countries.

Voters reject social democratic austerity

The management of the global financial crisis and eurozone crisis by social democratic governments was soon punished at the ballot box. As social democrats proposed more of the same, voters turned to other parties. A considerable chunk of centre-left voters turned to the Greens and parties of the radical left and a small proportion turned to the parties of the radical and/or populist right (Kitschelt & Häusermann 2021; Abou-Chadi & Wagner 2019). Thus, in the period following the 2008 global financial crisis, the electoral decline of social democratic parties intensified because of external shocks but mostly because of failures of imagination and ideological timidity (Rothstein & Steinmo 2013: 105). At the time, social democrats were, as Donald Sassoon argued, "idealess, as a remnant of the past facing an uncertain future" (2013: 27).

Demonstrating this ideological disorientation, the PES obtained only 27.2 per cent of the vote at the 2009 elections to the EP, while across the different European countries social democratic-led governments started to collapse. The German SPD was the first European social democratic party to lose elections in the wake of the global financial crisis. It lost the 2009 general elections (and consequently its role in the Christian Democratic Union-led coalition government that had been formed in 2005) and it struggled to attract more than 30 per cent share of the vote until the 2017 elections (Jun 2018: 103). In Britain, the Labour Party suffered a crushing defeat at the 2010 general election and has been in opposition ever since. In Sweden, the SAP scored its worst result since 1914, winning only 30.7 per cent of the vote at the 2010 general elections (Andersson 2016: 116). In Spain and Portugal, the socialist governments suffered devastating defeats in 2011 following draconian austerity measures demanded by the troika as part of a bailout agreement, in the case of Portugal, or demanded by the EU as part of a bank bailout programme, in the case of Spain (Kennedy 2016: 178; Ramos 2019: 62; Motos 2019: 34). In Greece, PASOK suffered a rout at the 2012 general election (it obtained only 12 per cent of vote) from which the party has not yet recovered.

In Italy, the eurozone crisis destabilized party politics. The right, led by Silvio Berlusconi, was in power for most of the economic crisis, but in 2011 it was replaced by a technocratic government led by Mario Monti which opened the way for greater social contestation and led to the emergence in 2013 of a new party, the Five Star Movement. This party posed a considerable challenge to the Democratic Party led by Pier Luigi Bersani.

At the 2013 elections, the Democratic Party was the most popular party, winning 29.6 per cent of the vote, while the newcomer the Five Star Movement captured 25.6 per cent of the vote. Bersani failed to form a government, but his successor Enrico Letta was able to form one thanks to the intervention of the President Giorgio Napolitano. Given the new electoral arithmetic and the fragile state of Italy's economy, the grand coalition government that was formed was not a recipe for political stability. By 2014, the Democratic Party had a new leader, the 'Third Wayer' Matteo Renzi, who formed a new government which he led until 2018 (Martín 2019: 104) but which was at the mercy of events. Since then, the Democratic Party has been in opposition.

In France, the socialist presidential candidate François Hollande won the elections in 2012 with a promise to turn the page on austerity and reform the eurozone. However, within months of taking office Hollande endorsed the eurozone's Fiscal Compact, which he had promised to renegotiate. The result of this endorsement was, of course, the continuation of austerity, as the Fiscal Compact committed the French government to obey the eurozone's fiscal rules and to produce a null structural deficit (Bouillard 2016: 155). In Ireland, the Labour Party tried to capitalize on the unpopularity of austerity by offering voters a choice between "Frankfurt's way or Labour's way" (Holmes 2019: 68). Labour's electoral gamble resulted in the party's best results in decades. But the failure to deliver on that promise resulted in Labour's third worst result in its history at the 2016 elections. Similarly, the Dutch

PvdA became the second largest party in parliament and joined again a coalition government with the centre-right People's Party for Freedom and Democracy, but in 2017 it suffered its worse electoral defeat ever, electing only nine MPs (Keman 2023: 148).

Clearly, the role of European social democratic governments in agreeing to and implementing draconian austerity measures played a key role in the electoral defeats suffered since the beginning of the global financial crisis. In most cases, social democratic governments were isolated or in the minority group of governments that had devised an austerity response to the crisis. It was only when the impact of the eurozone crisis and its flawed management became apparent that social democrats started to address its shortcomings. The then leader of the SPD, Sigmar Gabriel, claimed in 2011 that "we, Social Democrats are convinced that capitalism needs to be tamed a second time" (Gabriel quoted in Holmes & Roder 2019: 1), while the French and Italian governments tried to argue in favour of a vague idea of "social Europe", which at least turned the page on austerity. But theirs were lone voices in a mostly conservative EU.

The PES also started to gradually challenge the ordoliberal consensus of the EU. In a veiled critique to the management of the eurozone crisis, the PES sent an alternative troika to Greece in 2012 with the purpose of proposing a solution that balanced debt alleviation with a stimulus programme (Holmes & Lightfoot 2016: 223). The critique of the EU's management of the crisis was fleshed out in the manifesto for the 2014 EP elections, where the PES proposed reforms to the governance of the eurozone whereby national governments would be being given greater "room for manoeuvre for investments in national budgets and for the mutualisation of rights and responsibilities within the Eurozone" (PES 2014).

This stance disguised the divisions within the European social democratic family about the future direction of the monetary union. While the social democratic parties of southern Europe and France called for greater fiscal room to invest in infrastructure and skills and develop high-wage economies, the social democratic parties of northern Europe insisted on the need for tight fiscal discipline. The German SPD, which was part of a coalition government led by Angela Merkel, and the Dutch PvdA, did not question the need for fiscal rectitude at a time of crises (Roder 2019: 179). The Finnish social democrats changed their approach. If at the start of the eurozone crises they called for a more humane Europe and asked for the burden of the crisis to not be borne by citizens alone (Raunio 2019: 148), they ended up demanding harsh conditionalities in exchange for the bailouts awarded to Greece, Portugal and Ireland and in the partial bailout to Spain.

In Britain, the Labour leader Ed Miliband developed a programme that sought to turn the page on Third Way politics and renew the social democratic roots of the party. He declared that his mission was to tackle inequality, which had risen in the previous decade, and proposed a blueprint which sought to regulate financial markets and promote an active industrial policy, higher wages and better working conditions. He surrounded himself with policy experts and left-wing intellectuals and articulated a cogent narrative but he was not in control of the political agenda. Eventually, he succumbed to the pressure coming from the right of the party and from the media and proposed a lighter version of austerity. The result was an inconsistent party programme that did not impress voters at the 2015 general election (Goes 2016). His successor, Jeremy Corbyn, insisted on turning the page on austerity and proposed a similar, although redder, programme to Miliband's but he too was defeated in 2017 and 2019 (Goes 2018, 2020).

The anti-austerity turn of social democratic parties was a case of too little, too late. The proposals made by social democrats offered remedial succour, but they neither dealt with the structural causes of the global financial crisis and eurozone crisis nor did they tackle their effects. Indeed, the inadequate response to these crises resulted in a lost decade of growth for most Europeans, and in the deepening of social inequalities and poverty rates, which in turn exposed structural fragilities in the continent's economies and left profound social scars.

A world of polycrisis

If dealing with the aftershocks of the global financial crisis and the eurozone crisis was not hard enough, a new cycle of disparate but simultaneous and disorientating crises brought more disruption to European politics. The historian Adam Tooze called this phenomenon a polycrisis, whose distinguishing feature is how the different shocks of disparate crises interact with each other "so that the whole is more overwhelming than the sum of its parts" (2022). Its effects have created a growing sense of general insecurity and powerlessness among citizens and fed a politics of anger which has been detrimental to social democratic parties. Above all, the disconcerting speed at which these multiple crises have succeeded each other have left politicians and citizens disorientated since 2007.

As the eurozone crisis slowly faded into the background, the 2015 migration and refugee crisis revealed a divided and polarized Europe. Over five million refugees, mostly from Syria, Somalia, Eritrea and Afghanistan, arrived in Europe through the continent's most economically vulnerable gateways – Greece, Italy and Spain – but did not encounter a welcoming continent. Apart from Germany, who welcomed over one million refugees from Syria between 2015 and 2016, most European countries were unwilling to open the doors to the new wave of refugees. The Austrian, Polish and Hungarian governments, led by right-wing populist parties, loudly refused to host refugees from non-European backgrounds, but most European governments engaged in a game of "pass the parcel" which culminated in the EU outsourcing part of its international responsibilities towards refugees to Turkey and Tunisia.

The political impact of the refugee crisis was felt almost immediately. In Britain, the salience of the migration crisis in political debates was a key driver behind the vote to leave the EU in the referendum of 2016 (Evans & Menon 2017). In Germany, a new far-right party, Alternatif für Deutchsland, disrupted party politics by winning 94 seats at the 2017 legislative elections. In France, the far-right leader Marine le Pen was the second most popular candidate in the second round of the 2017 presidential elections, winning 33.9 per cent of the vote. The second notable fact of these elections was the pulverization of the Socialist Party and of the main party of the centre-right, Les Républicains.

The signs of a more fragmented and volatile political landscape were also visible in the result of the 2019 EP elections. The centre-right and centre-left party groupings lost their majority, while Eurosceptic and radical right parties elected a record number of MEPs (73 in total), and European Green parties and the alliance of liberal and pro-European parties also increased their representation.

While mainstream parties were still dealing with the impact of the eurozone and refugee crises, the politics of the climate emergency and its subsequent populist backlash pushed politicians in other directions.

The climate emergency expressed in extreme weather events alerted politicians and European citizens to the seriousness of the problem. However, the politics of the green transition was (and remains) divisive. While young people, mobilized by Greta Thunberg's campaign "Fridays for the Future", and intergenerational groups comprising mostly middle-class and urban citizens participated in the direct action activities of environmental social movements, suburban and less affluent voters were not supportive of policies which could result in higher living costs. This backlash against environmental policies was expressed in the rising popularity of radical right parties which questioned the seriousness of the climate emergency and was particularly visible in the mass "yellow vests" protests that paralysed France from 2018 to 2020.

Following the French government's decision to launch a new tax on fuel as a measure to tackle the climate emergency, thousands of protesters, first in the rural and suburban parts of France and then in its major cities, mobilized and took to the streets in often violent protests (Grossman & Mayer 2022). These "yellow vests" protests went on until a new crisis brought the world into lockdown. The global Covid-19 pandemic, which was first detected in the Chinese province of Wuhan in the final months of 2019, had spread to the entire planet by the spring of 2020. In response to the pandemic, national governments closed their borders, paralysed their economies and forced everyone – apart from key workers – indoors.

The speed at which the pandemic spread, and its dramatic death toll, alarmed European governments. The quest to save lives led European leaders to agree to spend millions of euros of public funds in an effort to keep national economies alive by subsiding wages, providing support to private companies and ensuring that health care systems had the medical resources required to fight the pandemic. By May 2020, the European Commission had announced a European Recovery Plan (ERP) worth €750 billion, which was designed to help EU member states to recover from the pandemic. In tandem with the ERP, European leaders announced the suspension of the eurozone governance rules. Both these measures reflected a recognition by European leaders that their response to the eurozone crisis had created more problems than it had solved.

By the time the pandemic stopped making headlines in 2022, it had exposed wide social and health inequalities as well as the impact of austerity over the capacity of health care systems and provoked a large popular backlash against lockdown measures, vaccination policies and science. Above all, the pandemic triggered, according to the World Bank, "the largest economic crisis in more than a century" and led to a "dramatic increase in inequality within and across countries" (World Bank 2022).

As the different European countries were still addressing the impact of the pandemic as well as the underlying problems it had revealed, Russia's invasion of Ukraine in February of 2022 plunged Europe into another crisis. The start of a war in Europe involving Russia had huge geopolitical and economic implications. If initially it was relatively easy to rhetorically condemn Russia for its act of aggression, European disagreements about the EU's response to the war soon became apparent. Those disagreements reflected not only different foreign policy priorities but above all different degrees of economic and energy dependence from Russia. As major economies such as Germany's scrambled to find alternative sources of energy to Russian natural gas, the rise in energy prices hit European economies like an electric shock.

Nonetheless, a month after the start of the conflict the EU agreed a packet of punitive sanctions against Russia, a plan to phase out member states' dependence on Russian fossil fuels and a strategy to mitigate the economic impact of the rise of inflation and energy prices. To avoid a recession, European governments committed themselves, with some variation, to subsidize energy prices for private consumers, reduce the consumption of energy and cap the revenues of energy providers. The package of measures announced prevented Europe from going into recession again, but it severely impacted economic performance across the continent.

If the different governments managed to find remedies that mitigated the effects of the succession of crises it was also clear that those solutions were a sticking plaster. But if some interpreted the polycrisis as a worldview that privileged technocracy, managerialism and what John Ganz defined as a "Keynesianism of despair" (2023), it also opened windows of opportunity to imagine a different political agenda where states have a more active and powerful role in the management of the world economy.

Ideas for a world transformed

Encouraged by the political and intellectual openness that the poly-crisis had inspired across the world, an abundance of policy propos-als and diagnoses were discussed in think tanks, in the mainstream media and in the wider ecosystem of scholars, public intellectuals and activists involved in developing and/or influencing social dem-ocratic programmes. Many of these ideas had the potential to renew social democracy as both a theory and a practice. Think tanks such as the Friedrich Ebert Foundation, the Karl Renner Institute, the Fabian Society, the Institute for Public Policy Research, to name a few, regularly published policy briefs and reports that proposed diagnostics and solu-tions for the disparate crises. At the European level, the Federation of European Progressive Studies (the research arm of the PES) mobilized scholars, researchers, trade unionists and parliamentarians to discuss ideas and draft proposals in round after round of the Next Left Agenda in the hope of influencing the programmatic agenda of European social democrats.

The ideas discussed ranged from ambitious proposals that tackled structural problems such as globalization, the climate emergency, euro-zone governance rules, a new approach to industrial and competition policies and the regulation of capitalism, to targeted policies that sought to address specific policy problems such as intergenerational injustice, labour precarity, the gender pay gap, racial inequality, the deepening of inequalities, democratic backsliding and the threats posed by automa-tion and artificial intelligence.

Most of these ideas had been in circulation in academic and policy circles for some time. Scholars such as Dani Rodrik had spent part of the previous decade suggesting reforms to tame globalization which included the incorporation of environmental, labour and consumer safety standards into world trade rules (2011: 255). But if in the past these suggestions had been politely heard but quietly dismissed, in the age of the polycrisis they were getting a hearing. If anything, the polycrisis of the twenty-first century showed that globalization was not a force of nature that could not be controlled or regulated. State intervention saved global capitalism during the global financial crisis. Moreover, during the pandemic the substantial reduction in global trade flows was accompanied by unprecedented state intervention in national economies which prevented Europe and the United States from plunging into deep and long economic recessions.

Given the socioeconomic impact of the eurozone crisis, the pandemic and the climate emergency, the realization that Europe's economic stagnation was mostly a result of lack of investment and that scientific innovations such as the Covid-19 vaccines had been possible thanks to substantial public investment led to changes to the EU's industrial and competition policies. Finally, in the United States and following the pandemic, the Biden administration's response to the rise of inflation and energy prices showed that the state had the power to shape markets, steer public investment to key areas of the economy and lead the green transition. Indeed, Biden's 2022 Inflation Reduction Act and the Chips and Science Act are seen as two of the most economically transformative pieces of legislation of the last 50 years in the United States.

Thus, proposals to develop a new and more active role for the state focused on two issues: the regulation of capitalism, especially of financial capitalism, with the purpose of promoting the public good (Martell 2012: 39); and the promotion of a new industrial strategy that recognized the role of the state in funding scientific and technological innovations and crucially in leading the transition to a carbon neutral economy, also known as "net zero". If the proposals to regulate financial markets were incremental and piecemeal in nature, the new industrial strategy based on Mariana Mazzucato's "entrepreneurial state"[1] (2013) or on Dani Rodrik's (2022) concept of "new productivism"[2] offered plausible proposals to initiate the transition to green economics, which represented a departure from the neoliberalism of the 1990s. This is so because these approaches propose more robust tools to discipline capital as well as activist industrial policies which depart from the market orthodoxies of the 1990s. This being said, there is a debate about the extent to which "Bidenomics" departs from neoliberalism (Amarnath *et al.* 2023). There are also differences in the way the USA, the EU and Britain develop their approaches to industrial policy and decarbonizing the economy.

In the EU the extent of change in thinking about economic policy is muddied by the eurozone governance rules. If the Next Generation programme and the EU's Green New Deal shows a willingness to think differently about the role of the state, there is still resistance to reform the governance rules of the eurozone. These rules not only constrain state capacity and reinforce and deepen regional inequalities but they also preclude, as Frederic Lordon put it, "any possibility of progressive policies" (2015). In this area, reform has been incremental at best. Some governments have proposed the creation of European funds which would be used to invest in infrastructure and innovation projects leading to a form of ordoliberalism at home and Keynesianism at the European level. To some extent, the EU's Next Generation recovery fund offers some help to national governments, although this fund is temporary. Where there is less agreement is about whether the eurozone rules should also include criteria that promote full employment and sustainable growth, and on granting greater national and democratic control over macroeconomic policy.

The European Commission presented its own proposals to reform the eurozone in 2022 with a view to loosening its fiscal rules and giving national governments greater fiscal space to invest in their own economic priorities. The Commission's proposals were supported by the social democratic governments of southern Europe and by France, but they encountered resistance from northern, eastern, central and Baltic European governments, including from social democratic governments. Nonetheless, a debate has started which shows that there is at least a recognition that the eurozone rules are an obstacle not only to social democratic politics but also to the future economic prosperity of Europe.

Alongside ideas to reimagine a new role for the state in industrial policy and to reform the eurozone, other proposals have been made to address what has been identified as the big problem of the age: the rise of inequality. In the hugely influential book *The Spirit Level: Why Equality Is Better for Everyone*, Richard Wilkinson and Kate Pickett (2009) were the first to warn about the impact of rising inequality on a range of variables, from life expectancy and crime to economic growth, health and educational outcomes, but others soon followed. Scholarly analysis of the dramatic rise of inequality by Thomas Piketty (2014) and Anthony Atkinson (2015) reached bestseller status. The International Monetary Fund and the Organisation for Economic Co-operation and Development wrote copious reports about the negative impact of inequality on economic growth and social cohesion (Stiglitz 2013), and the mainstream media discussed the rise of inequality on a regular basis in opinion columns, talk shows and popular podcasts. Bookending this debate, the political theorist Albena Azmanova suggested that the generalized sense of insecurity and precarity felt by citizens around the world was a more debilitating form of social injustice than the rise of inequalities (2020: 165).

Whether the problem was presented as inequality or insecurity, several ideas were intensely debated in political and policy circles as solutions to it. For a while the proposal to introduce a universal basic income (UBI) dominated policy debates (Finland even started a pilot project on UBI). However, the proposal to offer an unconditional basic income to all citizens was eventually discarded by most social democratic parties who felt it was both unaffordable and ideologically complicated. After all, social democratic parties have been historically associated with the labour movement and the promotion of full employment. For those reasons, left-wing intellectuals and social democratic activists were keener to support proposals to either create a job guarantee (Mitchell & Fazi 2017: 241) or universal basic services as alternatives to UBI.

Other ideas gained wide currency in social democratic circles which had a long lineage in social democratic thinking. It was by now clear that the rise in inequalities and the decline in support for social democratic parties were strongly correlated with the decline of trade unions (Montebello *et al.* 2022). The decline in the power of trade unions was in turn correlated with the rise of insecure and precarious work, especially among the young. Thus, as the Guild Socialists in Britain, the Swedish social democrats and the Austro-Marxists had proposed in the 1920s, and Kreisky, Brandt and Palme promoted in the 1970s, left-leaning intellectuals started to defend economic democracy, greater employment rights and stronger trade unions, as well as ideas on collective (or cooperative) ownership of economic assets as the necessary countervailing power to globalized capital.

These ideas took on different shapes. For example, Thomas Piketty proposed "participatory socialism", which he defined as "a new universalist egalitarian perspective based on social ownership, education, and shared knowledge and power" (2020: 967). Piketty's participatory socialism included proposals such as new forms of social ownership of economic assets, a wealth tax, economic democracy and a UBI. Similarly, Martin O'Neill, Thad Williamson and their team of scholars explored the Rawlsian idea of a "property-owning democracy" based on a political economy characterized by a "wide dispersal of capital with the political capacity to block the very rich and corporate elites from dominating the economy and relevant public policies" (2014: 4). And in a widely discussed book, Daniel Chandler proposed, among other ideas, the expansion of "workplace democracy" or "co-management" (2023: 256).

The belief that economic power had to be more evenly distributed in society was the common thread uniting these different proposals. One of the most effective ways to achieve this was to promote higher rates of trade union membership and stronger collective bargaining mechanisms, as well the greater involvement of workers in the management of companies. Economic democracy also required stronger redistributive policies that targeted wealth inequality rather than income inequality. Thus, social democratic proposals for fiscal policy started to focus on creating wealth taxes, closing tax havens and tackling tax evasion.

In short, the multiple crises that have hit Europe stimulated debates and generated ideas and policy proposals that had the potential to revitalize social democracy. However, endorsing and implementing new ideas is difficult. Most contemporary social democratic leaders were politicized in the age of neoliberalism and Third Way politics. Thus, the support for new ideas requires an intellectual leap of faith. Moreover, social democratic parties are operating in a radically different political and economic environment from the past and which is characterized by highly fragmented and polarized party systems and stagnating economies. If there are ideas that can contribute to the ideological revitalization of social democracy, it is not clear whether a majority of disillusioned European voters would support them.

Explaining the faint social democratic recovery

Nonetheless, social democrats have started to engage with some of these ideas. As Rob Manwaring showed, there has been a considerable movement leftwards in the programmes of social democratic parties since 2010 (2021: 71). They have placed the promotion of egalitarian policies and of the green transition, as well as more investment in public services and in the development of the market-making and market-shaping capacity of states, at the centre of their agendas. In addition, eurozone reform and a "social Europe" have been back on the agenda since the pandemic. Even the German SPD led by Olaf Scholz recognized the need to reform the eurozone with a view to promoting greater economic convergence across Europe, although once in government he supported the "ordoliberal" stances of his liberal coalition partner.

In some parts of the continent this leftward shift was rewarded at the ballot box. The slow and faint revival of social democratic electoral fortunes started in October of 2015, when the Portuguese PS led by António Costa managed to snatch victory from the jaws of defeat. Instead of joining the centre-right in a coalition government, Costa decided to form a quasi-coalition government with the Communist Party, the Green Party and the Left Bloc. The four parties were united in the purpose of reversing most of the public-spending cuts (namely to wages and pensions) that were demanded by the troika and introduced by the centre-right government in the period 2011–15. Costa has also been highly critical of the eurozone rules and has consistently campaigned with like-minded European governments for their reform.

The electoral and political success of the quasi-coalition government led by Costa – colloquially known as the Contraption (*Gerigonça*) – was an inspiration to some social democratic parties for both its focus on turning the page on austerity and for the fruitful partnership between the parties of the left. However, its achievements were modest. Although there were noticeable rises to the minimum wage, pensions, public sector wages and welfare support to families, public services continued to suffer from severe underfunding. Nonetheless, Costa's PS managed to win two more elections and achieved the rare feat of winning a landslide victory at the 2022 general elections. But Costa's luck run out when a corruption scandal led to his resignation from government and to the calling of early elections in November 2023.

The relative success of the Portuguese PS offered some hope to the European left. Costa's Contraption template was eventually picked up by the Spanish PSOE in 2018. Following years of political instability, the PSOE had to adapt to a new party system with strong new parties that covered the whole of the political spectrum, from the radical left to the centre to the far-right. The fragmentation of the party system at a time of successive crises resulted in four elections and several minority governments in a period of five years. Following a confidence motion against the conservative government, Pedro Sánchez was appointed prime minister in 2018, and in late 2019 he won the Spanish elections which enabled him to form a government with the support of a coalition of left-wing parties named Unidas Podemos (which fought the 2023 general elections under the name Movimiento Sumar) and was able to cling on to power following the inconclusive 2023 elections.[3] This coalition government was able to introduce a range of progressive proposals, namely labour market reforms that tackle work insecurity and precarity, subsidies to encourage the use of public transport and targeted value-added tax cuts to address the cost-of-living crisis, as well as an ambitious programme to decarbonize the economy (Cliffe 2023). Nonetheless, the electoral successes of the Iberian social democrats were built on fragile electoral coalitions that might crumble suddenly.

In Germany, the SPD led by Olaf Scholz narrowly won the 2021 legislative elections with 25.7 per cent share of the vote, following a campaign that sought to turn the page on the labour reforms of Gerhard

Portuguese prime minister Antonio Costa (*left*) meets with visiting Spanish prime minister Pedro Sanchez in Lisbon, July 2018

Source: Xinhua / Alamy Stock Photo.

Schröder by promising, in a move inspired by the philosopher Michael Sandel's critique of meritocracy, to restore the "dignity of work" and respect for workers. Following a few months of negotiations, the social democrats formed an unlikely and not necessarily stable coalition government with the Greens and the Free Democratic Party.

Social democrats also made a comeback in Sweden, Finland, Norway and Denmark, although in some cases this was short-lived. In Norway, the Labour Party returned to power in 2021 after eight years on the opposition benches. In Sweden, the SAP returned to power in 2018 after a parliamentary term in opposition, but on a much lower share of vote. As a result, the social democrats managed to form a minority coalition government with the Greens, and with the support of the Liberals and the Centre Party, for important bills such as the approval of the annual budget but in exchange for "neoliberal reforms" (Oskarson 2023: 84). However, and despite winning the largest share of votes, the social democrats returned to the opposition benches in 2022 following the electoral breakthrough of the Sweden Democrats, which became the second largest party in Swedish parliament (at the expense of the centre-right party), although popular discontent with deteriorating public services and the cost-of-living crisis (and not immigration) were the main drivers of the defeat. These results were especially disappointing as the SAP's new leader, Magdalena Andersson, tried to revive the party's old social democratic roots by promising to the tackle social inequalities and decarbonize the economy (Oskarson 2021).

Similarly, in Finland the social democrats were voted out of power in 2023 following a period of four years leading the government. By contrast, the Danish Social Democrats bucked the trend and won the 2019 legislative elections, although this result followed the party's endorsement of restrictive immigration policies in an attempt to win over working-class voters (Nedergaard 2023: 177–8). What is clear is that in northern Europe, social democratic parties no longer command the support they were historically associated with. The neoliberal reforms to the labour market and the welfare state and partial privatization of public services that were introduced in the 1990s and early 2000s led to the loss of many working-class voters while new migratory flows from outside Europe paved the way for the rise of far-right parties.

In Italy, the Democratic Party continued to fragment into short-lived new left-wing formations. This meant that the social democratic left has been unable to win an election since it was voted out of office in 2018. In France, the PSF was nearly annihilated following Emmanuel Macron's election in 2017 presidential election (Klemperer 2022). La France Insoumise (France Unbowed), led by the left-wing populist Jean-Luc Mélenchon, and the Greens became the most popular parties of the left. In 2022, the PS reached a new low when the socialist presidential candidate Anne Hidalgo won only 1.8 per cent of the vote.

In the Netherlands, the PvdA was also decimated at the 2017 legislative elections. The party's defeat has been interpreted as a sign of an identity crisis that had been going on for some time and which was characterized by the party's inability to develop a social democratic programme. But the PvdA's unpopularity is also a result of the popular reaction to the austerity path it supported while in government (Oudenampsen 2021: 42). In any case, what became clear after the 2017 elections is that the PvdA's revival could not rely on the pursuit of the elusive median voter given that party politics are now even more fragmented than in the past.

In Austria, the SPÖ had been trailing in the opinion polls since the 2015 migration crisis and lost the 2017 general election. That defeat led to a period of reflection and renewal. In 2018 the party adopted a new manifesto, which endorsed ideas of economic democracy, and which asserted that "financial markets must never again become independent in this form" (SPÖ quoted by Sandner 2023: 141). Since 2023, the new leader, Andreas Babler has been steering the party in a clear social democratic path.

In Britain, the Labour Party has been in opposition since 2010 and lost a total of four elections. This period in opposition was marked by high political turbulence. Following the global financial crisis, the public voted to leave the EU and participated in three more general elections (in 2015, 2017 and 2019). In this turbulent period, different party leaders tried a variety of strategies, but none resulted in electoral victory. Since 2020, the party, under the leadership of Keir Starmer, has revived the New Labour strategy of the 1990s (Diamond 2023: 60) by focusing on demonstrating economic competence by keeping conservative public-spending plans, ruling out raising wealth and income taxes and defending harsh immigration and law-and-order stances.

In eastern and central Europe, social democracy is in deeper trouble. Except for Czechia, where the social democrats led or participated in government until 2018, social democracy has been out of power in the region for more than a decade. In Latvia, the unpopularity of the social democrats is so striking that the party Latvian Social Democratic Workers' Party was demoted to observer status in the Socialist International and in the PES. And in Hungary and Slovakia, the populist right has dominated politics for over a decade. The constitutional reforms these right-wing governments introduced have made it more difficult for weak social democratic parties to dislodge the populist right from office.

In short, the successive crises that European countries experienced since 2008 have contributed to greater polarization and to the intensification of the fragmentation of party system, which has been ongoing since the 1990s. These two phenomena have been hugely detrimental to European social democracy. As European social democratic parties have found since 2010, combining the right policy mixes and narratives that can result in a winning electoral formula is quite challenging, especially when party leaders are somewhat distanced from their activist base and seem to have forgotten the historic mission their ideological tradition represents.

Social democracy in fragmented party systems

As explained above, there is variation in the electoral performance of social democratic parties which can be explained by the varied pace of political and economic change, the different electoral systems used across Europe and, of course, national path-dependent features. Nonetheless, across the European continent social democratic parties have struggled electorally, and in the cases where they have been in power, they are no longer the hegemonic force of the European left they once were.

What seems clear is that the programmatic changes initiated in the 1990s, namely the endorsement of neo-revisionist social democracy, contributed to that decline. The rightwards shift of social democratic parties, which in the short-term produced impressive electoral successes, contributed to the electoral losses suffered since the early 2000s. Indeed, the electoral coalition of voters that led to the Third Way wave collapsed as a result of two factors. First, the electoral support of university-educated, middle-class and urban voters was unreliable. This type of voter tends to be more fickle in their voting behaviour than the working-class voters that had constituted the core vote of social democratic parties in the postwar period (Karreth *et al.* 2012: 792).

Second, the rightwards shift of social democratic parties drove away many core voters who shifted their allegiances to other left-wing parties (Karreth *et al.* 2012: 815; Bremer & Rennwald 2022: 3; Polacko 2022). This phenomenon was particularly visible in countries with proportional representation systems and with relatively strong parties of the radical left or green parties. In the case of Greece, the radical left party Syriza replaced PASOK as the party of social democratic voters; in Germany the SPD suffered because of the emergence of the new party of the left, Die Linke, in 2005 and crucially because of the rise of the Greens (Menz 2023: 64) and in France the radical left La France Insoumise led by Jean-Luc Mélenchon as well as the Green Party have eaten away a substantial chunk of the electoral support for the socialists.

As explained in Chapter 3, the loss of core voters has been a long-term process which was intensified by the shift to a post-industrial economy, which in turn led to the shrinking of the unionized working class. But that decline is also a result of the passive acceptance by social democratic parties of the decline of trade unions. This latter point is particularly important given that the strongest indicator of electoral support for social democratic parties is trade union membership. As Bremer and Rennwald showed, "trade union members are 7.3 per cent more likely to support social democratic parties than non-members" (2022: 7). Historically, trade unions politicized and mobilized substantial groups of voters. However, the decline in trade union membership, which was accelerated by the Third Way approach to labour market reforms, meant that social democratic parties lost a significant share of their core vote, perhaps forever (Escalona & Vieira 2016: 37).

To fully grasp the causes of this electoral decline it is important to understand how those once reliable social democratic voters changed their party allegiances and voting preferences. Several studies have shown that most of the losses experienced by social democratic parties in the last two decades have been to mainstream centre-right parties and to parties of the left. Indeed, losses to green and radical left parties amount to almost 50 per cent of all vote losses of European social democratic parties (Häusermann *et al.* 2021: 2; Kitschelt & Häusermann 2021: 3–4). To make matters worse, when those voters switch to Green or radical left parties they tend to not come back to the social democratic fold in the following elections (Kitschelt & Häusermann 2021: 2).

Many of the voters who stopped supporting social democratic parties stopped voting altogether. Contrary to some popular (Eatwell & Goodwin 2018) accounts, working-class voters did not shift *en masse* to parties of the radical right. Research by Abou-Chadi *et al.* showed that only about 15 per cent of working-class voters have been supporting radical right parties in western Europe (2021: 16; Häusermann *et al.* 2021: 3), and of this percentage not all these working-class voters had voted for social democratic parties in the past. In fact, some working-class voters have always supported parties on the right (Abou-Chadi *et al.* 2021: 10). Confirming this trend, Polacko has also found that "the rightward economic movements of social democrats, significantly reduces their support under high levels of income inequality, or when they are combined with rightward socio-cultural movements" (2022: 684). In truth, many of those working-class voters shifted allegiances to the radical left, as many of them hold progressive views on LGBTQ+ issues, while a large share holds progressive or neutral (and therefore not very strong) attitudes to immigration (Abou-Chadi *et al.* 2021: 15).

In this new electoral landscape, social democratic parties face important dilemmas. Building a winning electoral coalition implies trade-offs, as attracting one group of voters can lead to the loss of another. For these reasons, Kitschelt and Häusermann argue that in the highly fragmented party systems of the twenty-first century the pursuit of catch-all strategies is no longer viable, especially in countries with proportional representation electoral systems (2021: 2). In countries that use plurality or majoritarian electoral systems, catch-all strategies may still be successful.

In these circumstances, the road to power may involve an electoral strategy that targets the specific groups of voters that can potentially give social democrats a majority or plurality at legislative elections. To start with, they should try to mobilize some of the core voters they lost in the last two decades. As Bremer and Rennwald explained, "though the number of demobilized supporters is not huge, appealing to these voters could be one easy way to slow down the electoral decline of social democracy" (2022: 10).

But this is not an easy task given that different groups of voters are heterogeneous in nature. For example, the political preferences of working-class voters are largely shaped by their position in the labour market (as insiders or outsiders), whether they work in industry or in services and whether they are unionized (Abou-Chadi *et al.* 2021: 15). Similarly, urban and university-educated graduates in middle-class occupations are not a homogenous voting group. Some can turn against redistributive policies, especially if they are combined with authoritarian/nationalist positions (Loxbo *et al.* 2019; Abou-Chadi & Wagner 2019: 1414).

Seen in this light, social democratic parties have an interest in developing an electoral coalition that includes the growing groups of urban professionals, working-class outsiders and the unionized working class by focusing on a left-wing economic agenda. After all, it was the ideological convergence between social democrats and the centre-right on economic policy that moved political competition to issues such as immigration and authoritarian values; areas where there are still significant differences between left and right parties (Polacko 2022: 685). On the other hand, the pursuit of centrist strategies is risky, given that for each centre-right voter that a centrist strategy might deliver it can result in the loss of more than one voter to the radical left or the greens (Kitschelt & Häusermann 2021: 3–4). Similarly, pursuing a strategy that chases voters with anti-immigration or nativist views is "not likely to result in electoral gains that would outweigh potential losses" (Abou-Chadi *et al.* 2021: 25).

But this is not a risk-free strategy in all national contexts. The electoral performance of social democratic parties in northern Europe, in Spain and in Britain offer some cautionary lessons which need to be unpacked. In countries such as Sweden, Finland and Denmark, anti-immigration, nativist and authoritarian views rose in saliency, contributing to the rise of far-right parties in the elections held in the last two decades.

The Danish Social Democrats have managed to get re-elected thanks in part to their restrictive immigration and asylum policies. In Sweden, the social democrats still received the most votes in the 2022 elections, but the rise of the far-right Sweden Democrats as the second largest party changed the electoral arithmetic. This change was compounded by the fact that the parties that had been part of the coalition government with the social democrats had disappointing results. However, the popularity of the Sweden Democrats is mostly because of popular discontent with the cost-of-living crisis and less with anti-immigration stances. In Spain, party politics cannot be disentangled from the country's conflicting nationalisms. The newcomer far-right party Vox emerged in reaction to the rise of Catalan nationalism, which culminated in the illegal 2014 referendum on independence. The fact that the PSOE relies on the support of Catalan and Basque nationalist parties did not escape the calculations of Vox and of the centre-right Partido Popular. If concerns with the cost-of-living crisis are added to the nationalist caldron, the result is an extremely volatile electoral dynamic that threatens the PSOE's long-term electoral prospects. Similarly, in Britain the electoral misfortunes of Labour since 2015 have been associated with voter concerns regarding immigration and with the party's competence to manage the economy. Indeed, in Labour's historical heartlands voters supported Brexit and elected conservative MPs at the 2019 general election. These few examples show that developing a programme that proves to be a lasting, winning electoral formula, addresses the many policy challenges voters consider important and renews the social democratic creed remains the holy grail of European social democracy.

Unfinished story

European social democracy has celebrated more than 160 years in politics. However, it is not clear whether it is a political ideology and practice that will survive, let alone shape, another century of European politics. Currently, European social democracy still shows vital signs but is on life support. In some cases – in Greece, France, Latvia, Poland and Hungary – social democracy is moribund, while in others the recovery has been slow, faint and short-lived. In other cases, social democratic parties still use the symbols and occasionally the language of social democracy, although it is not clear whether what they practice can be defined as social democratic. Interestingly, the new parties of the radical left that have either emerged or modernized in Spain, Greece, Portugal, France and elsewhere seem to be the new standard-bearers of social democratic values and policies of the postwar period. They are committed to social justice, the elimination of all inequalities, the regulation of capitalism and support for the welfare state.

By contrast, the historical political representatives of European social democracy seem to be too weak politically and too ideologically disorientated to guarantee its survival. Their programmes offer remedial solutions to the cost-of-living crisis, rising inequality, insecurity and slow growth, but they leave unaddressed the causes of those problems. For these reasons, the fourth act of social democracy remains unfinished and open-ended. It is up to the agents of social democracy – political parties, trade unions and activists – to determine how its story will end. This act can finish with another decade or so of proposing remedial solutions to important societal problems, which will amount to the transformation of social democracy into a hybrid ideology, or it can finish with a robust commitment to an emancipatory and transformative agenda. Whichever path social democrats choose, it will depend on the ideological conviction, courage, political shrewdness and sense of historic opportunity felt collectively by European social democrats.

Conclusion: an open future

Social democracy started as a social movement in the factories, working men's clubs, coffee-houses, newsrooms and streets of European urban centres, but by the late nineteenth century it was "captured" by newly created social democratic parties which sought to take advantage of universal suffrage as the new tool to achieve socialist ends. Over the following 160 years or so, the actions and choices of social democratic parties shaped our understanding of social democracy. But that capture never meant "ownership". Although the terms of doctrinal debates were largely set by social democratic parties, socialist intellectuals and activists developed the "set texts" of social democracy and closely monitored whether they were adhered to by the different parties. Occasionally intellectuals and activists were able to stop the pursuit of a certain path, or to force the inclusion of a policy goal. With the passing of time the tension in the relationship between political parties and intellectuals and activists became more acute, to the point where it is no longer certain whether social democratic parties practice social democracy.

The primacy of social democratic parties over activists and intellectuals does not mean the former controlled events and therefore their destinies. As Marx suggested in "The Eighteenth Brumaire of Louis Bonaparte", men make their own history but not in "circumstances they choose for themselves" (1996 [1875]: 38). In this constrained environment, social democratic parties had to work with the tools they encountered. In the late nineteenth century, those tools were male universal suffrage, and they too forced a course of action which was consequential. As Przeworski (1993) argued, choosing the parliamentary road to socialism meant prioritizing the short-term goal of winning elections over the long-term goal of overthrowing capitalism and developing a socialist society. This choice also meant that the socialist conquering of political power would be democratic.

Choosing this path to socialism was challenging. Universal male suffrage (and least of all universal suffrage) was not yet a reality across Europe and winning elections was fraught with difficulties. The working classes, in all their rich variety which included artisans, farm labourers, factory workers, office clerks and the new class of intellectuals who lived hand-to-mouth existences in the New Grub Streets[1] of European cities, did not constitute a majority of the electorate. Even when they constituted a numerical majority, the working classes were not a political majority, because they were not a homogenous group. Not all workers aspired to a socialist classless society shaped by bonds of cooperation. Many aspired to a bourgeois lifestyle; others simply wanted a general improvement to their working and living conditions. And even among those workers who aspired to a socialist society, there were those who prioritized incremental but immediate improvements to their living conditions over the promise of a socialist revolution.

The acceptance that social democratic parties needed to attract the support of voters who aspired to different conceptions of society was visible in the writings of Marx and Engels and in the resolutions of the Second International where they discussed the "agrarian question". This awareness led to a tweaking of social democratic strategies. To attract a broader coalition of voters, social democrats started to tone down ideological language and to emphasize instead the immediate material difference their policies would bring to voters' lives. Social democrats also had to learn how to use parliamentary democracy for their purposes. And learning about parliamentary procedures and building coalitions of allies to get pieces of legislation approved took time away from strategizing the socialist revolution.

Alongside the constraints imposed by the choice of pursuing a parliamentary path to socialism, social democrats, now sitting in parliaments, had to respond to the many crises they encountered. Economic recessions, wars, revolutions and the occasional big crisis of capitalism forced European social democrats to improvise, revise and adapt their political strategies and doctrines to respond to the circumstances they encountered on the ground.

This process was expected by the early theoreticians of socialism. From Marx to Kautsky, from Jaurès to Hilferding, social democrats knew that adapting to different political, economic and social circumstances was part of the journey to a socialist society. They were also aware that capitalism was a highly adaptable economic system. The only possible response to the adaptability of capitalism was not a detailed plan to destroy it, which in any case socialist theorists had failed to produce, but improvisation, layering and borrowing from other traditions. In this process of adaptation to external circumstances and immediate goals, social democracy proved to be a highly mouldable ideology.

This was a surprising outcome to those who expected social democracy to be a political movement and ideology that faithfully followed the canonical texts of socialism. As Tony Wright eloquently put it, "socialism was not seen as a mansion with many rooms, but as a house of theory and practice in which dissenting traditions were shown the door" (1996: 2). But, perhaps because of the immense constraints it encountered and the path-dependent way it developed across the continent, European social democracy became that mansion with many rooms which housed a variety of social democratic theories and practices. It was from the different historical trajectories, political traditions and heated disagreements about the ends and means of socialism that a variety of social democracies emerged in Europe.

In all its varieties, the transformation of social democracy followed a path-dependent process. The unique circumstances in which each social democratic party emerged shaped its future development. More crucially, allegiance to specific social democratic doctrines and values kept social democratic parties tied to a sometimes tenuous but always present set of values and aims. Nonetheless, social democracy changed because circumstances external to the movement forced social democrats to adapt, revise, transform and sometimes abandon traditional values or assumptions about how the world worked. Some of the changes were incremental and amounted to contextual adaptations that were almost imperceptible to the naked eye, but others, often resulting from external shocks, were transformational.

The relevance of doctrine resulted in the development of a specific pattern of transformation. To the key texts and principles of social democracy others were added like layers in a cake. While social democratic parties added new layers to social democrat doctrine, they quietly, and occasionally loudly, abandoned others in a process called drift. Change also happened through processes of conversion and displacement. By adapting (i.e., converging) (1) to the requirements of a capitalist economy and (2) to the neoliberal policies of the EU, social democratic parties displaced traditional social democratic means and ends.

Eventually, the result of this continuous layering, drifting, conversion, displacement (Streeck & Thelen 2010) and adaptation to external shocks was a radical transformation of the theory and, consequently, of the practice of social democracy. From a theory and practice that started with a commitment to the emancipation of workers in a socialist society, today European social democracy offers the promise of an individualistic form of self-reliance (and support to the vulnerable) required to live in a highly competitive capitalist society.

Either incremental or transformative, the process of change was protracted and slow. There were, as this volume suggests, four distinct phases or acts in the lifetime of European social democracy. Each phase gradually distanced social democracy from its original theories and values. In each of them, social democratic doctrine was taken seriously, and as a result the processes of change and transformation – tellingly defined as "revisionist" by activists and intellectuals – were experienced more as a moment of loss than a moment of renewal. But each revisionism, which sought to synch the doctrine with the practice, profoundly transformed social democracy.

Social democracy in theory and practice

To illustrate this point about the disjunction between theory and practice, it is worth examining the influence Karl Marx and Friedrich Engels over the social democratic movement. Both Marx and Engels used *The Communist Manifesto* of 1848 to set up a rough road map to a socialist society led by the workers' movement organized in political parties. This easily digestible call to arms influenced the foundation of the German SPD, which in turn shaped the social democratic parties that emerged in Europe in the late nineteenth century as well as the principles of the Second International. However, in other writings – for example, the "The Class Struggle in France" or "The Eighteenth Brumaire of Louis Bonaparte" – Marx seemed to suggest that the socialist revolution was a long-term project whose beginning was conditional on the existence of a capitalist economy and a politically conscious proletariat committed to the socialist revolution who would overthrow capitalism and set up a socialist society.

But Marx was not always so patient or tolerant of other interpretations of the revolutionary creed. His fights with Bakunin, which culminated in the collapse of the First International, and his rows with Louis Blanc in France or with the followers of Ferdinand Lassalle over the SPD's Gotha Programme, show that Marx believed his own interpretation of history and of the future of the socialism was the only acceptable one. Similarly, Engels, who at times had been eager to make the movement open to a variety of socialist traditions, became the guardian of Marxist orthodoxy within the social democratic movement. However, neither Marx or Engels disowned any of the parties or factions who were too bourgeois for their own liking. In fact, each of them maintained regular and supportive correspondence with the leaders of the newly formed social democratic parties.

Marx's and Engels's disputes with the different European social democratic parties show that their words were not treated as holy texts by the wider social democratic movement. In France, Jean Jaurès claimed "to be closer by heart and by reason to a republican, however moderate", than "to so-called Socialists" who do not see that "socialism was inherent in the republican movement from the outset" (2021 [1899]: 6). In a similar vein, the Fabian Society challenged Marx's account of capitalist wage exploitation, the concept of class struggle and the movement's revolutionary strategy[2] and proposed instead a "gradual transition" to social democracy which would involve a "socialist permeation of liberalism" and would culminate in the "transfer of rent and interest to the State, not in one lump sum, but by instalments" (Shaw 1961: 43). Even within the SPD, whose Gotha Programme was avowedly Marxist, there was dissention between the different followers of Marxism. Marx himself deplored the influence of Ferdinand Lassalle in the party's understanding of the value of labour and the role of the state (Marx 1996 [1875]: 222). And later, the revisionist crisis triggered by Bernstein's critique of Marxism in the late 1890s is another example of the disjunction between theory and practice.

The four acts of social democracy

Thus, disagreements about socialist doctrine became the bread and butter of social democratic politics and shaped the first act of social democracy. There were heated debates about the end goals of social democracy. Whether Marx and Engels as well as the resolutions of the Second International referred to the emancipation of the proletariat in a socialist society as their goal, other social democrats debated whether equality or fraternity or fellowship were the cardinal goals of socialism and whether these goals could be achieved in a capitalist society. More recently, social democrats refer to greater equality as the ultimate goal of socialism, but interestingly, as explained in the Introduction, neither Marx nor Engels were keen on this language.

European social democrats disagreed too about the means to develop a socialist society. They first debated whether reformism was acceptable, whether parliamentary democracy was a form of "dictatorship of the proletariat",[3] whether collaboration with bourgeois parties aided their cause and whether capitalism was favourable to the emancipation of the proletariat. But the first big and divisive debate was about the revolutionary path to socialism.

Marx and Engels established that revolution was necessary, but they never specified what they meant by that. It was not clear if they thought violence was required. If they believed violence could erupt (as they did in *The Communist Manifesto*), they also argued (especially after the violent crushing of the Paris Commune in 1871) that a revolution could amount to a radical but non-physically violent transformation of society. Interestingly, Engels described the dictatorship of the proletariat as the working class coming to power "under the form of the democratic Republic" (1934 [1891]: 486) and claimed that legal tactics were more effective than the "street fighting" normally used in "bourgeois revolutions" (1978 [1895]: 567–9). On the other hand, Lenin and Rosa Luxembourg claimed that a revolution was essential for the socialist cause.

This disagreement was the precursor to the first schism in the social democratic family and announced the end of the first act of social democracy. Following the Bolshevik Revolution of 1917, social democracy became an ideology and practice that only applied to those who pursued socialism via the parliamentary road. If there were a revolution, this one would be either led democratically by the workers' movement at some time in the future, as the Austro-Marxists defended, or it would be carried out "by peaceful, legal, and moral means, instead of by physical force", as Kautsky suggested (1988 [1918]: 93). This stance contrasted with the elite or vanguard rule defended by the Bolsheviks.

Social democrats disagreed too about the role of the state in the economy and the meaning of the concept of "workers' control of the means of production". If Marx and Engels had argued for the temporary state control of the means of production during the period of "dictatorship of the proletariat", British and German social democrats interpreted that expression to mean the permanent state control of industries and economic assets; the Guild Socialists, Austro-Marxists and Swedish social democrats preferred to talk of the socialization of the means of production and defended a democratic, bottom-up, cooperative economic system which would preferably exist alongside a social democratic state, but which could coexist with capitalism. However, they did agree (at least until the 1950s) that capitalism was an exploitative and unjust system of economic production that had to be overthrown at some undefined time in the future.

The accommodation to capitalism, which defined the second act of social democracy, started in the early twentieth century with Bernstein's revisionist thesis, but it only became a doctrinal point in the late 1950s. In the meantime, social democrats muddled through the Great Depression of the 1930s and postwar reconstruction by occasionally accepting the orthodoxies of modern capitalist economies.

This process of accommodation also included innovative approaches to the economy that radically transformed the character of capitalism. Sweden's SAP was the first social democratic party to experiment with economic policies that prioritized full employment and social justice. Soon other parties copied or adapted that approach. By the 1950s capitalism was a much tamer beast. In many European countries, governments had nationalized key economic assets, created and developed robust welfare states which offered protection from cradle to grave, promoted full employment and heavily taxed private profits and top incomes.

This radical transformation of capitalism informed social democratic attitudes to it. As Anthony Crosland noticed in the 1950s, the new capitalism was radically different from the one that Marx had described. It was a capitalism that socialists could not only live with but use to achieve socialist ends. The economic growth generated by regulated capitalist production enabled social democrats to redistribute wealth, strengthen welfare states, promote solidarity and contribute to the emancipation of all workers. The SPD's Bad Godesberg's motto, "as much competition as possible – as much planning as necessary", was emblematic of that change.

The third act of social democracy came about when tamed capitalism was no longer generating the high levels of economic growth experienced in the 1950s and 1960s. The collapse of the Bretton Woods international financial system and the oil shocks of the 1970s, alongside inflation, stagflation and economic globalization, challenged the validity of the social democratic formula "Keynesianism plus welfare state". Gradually, social democrats started to accept, as Berman argued, the primacy of markets over politics (2006). In other words, instead of regulating capitalism to achieve socialist aims, social democrats accepted the fiscal discipline imposed by markets. As they accepted that globalization could not be challenged or redirected towards other goals, social democratic programmes focused instead on creating the conditions for more economic growth (whose proceeds would enable investments in education, the welfare state and other public services), in offering remedial solutions to poverty and in preparing workers to compete in the global capitalist economy.

Instead of tamed capitalism, which was mediated and regulated by the state, the new capitalism demanded light regulation of financial markets, fiscal discipline, low taxes and the erosion of welfare states and social rights as the conditions to generate economic growth. This also involved the acceptance that market values would not limit themselves to the economic sphere and would permeate all areas of public life. More seriously, this uncritical embrace of capitalism and economic competition moved social democratic parties further away from their goal of human emancipation in a cooperative society. In short, without realizing it social democrats were reversing the reforms that had made the acceptance of capitalism not only possible but doctrinally compatible with the goals of social democracy. For this reason, the third act was consequential because it changed not only the means but also the ends of social democracy.

The fourth act of social democracy has been mostly about social democrats coming to terms with the consequences of their acceptance of the primacy of markets. By the beginning of the twenty-first century, deregulated capitalism was no longer generating high rates of economic growth. Instead, it was producing high levels of inequality, insecurity and regular recessions that were both small, such as the dot.com boom in the early 2000s, and big, such as the global financial crisis of 2008.

During this fourth act, social democrats have been mostly disorientated. The successive crises left them, again, without an economic policy. Alongside the problems of rising inequalities and economic instability, social democrats faced new and difficult problems. The climate emergency was one challenge that questioned economic policies geared to generate a form of economic growth based on higher production and consumption levels. The pandemic of 2020 showed that the several rounds of austerity implemented in the previous decade left states with threadbare healthcare systems and public services. Overwhelmed by the impact of so many crises, social democrats have switched between muddling through, proposing a bit of higher spending here or a technocratic intervention there, and searching for ambitious and transformative solutions which could renew the social democratic creed both in terms of doctrines and practice.

Interestingly, the transformation and dilution of social democracy is correlated with the declining influence of socialist intellectuals over social democratic parties. As observed by Mudge (2018), the theorists of social democracy slowly lost their influence over social democratic parties. If at the turn of the nineteenth century, social democratic parties had their own, self-taught and rigorous working-class intellectuals (Bernstein and Kautsky are two examples), and by the mid-twentieth century social democratic parties were influenced by professional and ideologically sympathetic economists, by the twenty-first century the figure of the intellectual had mostly disappeared from social democratic parties. If in the twenty-first century party leaders like to claim they are influenced by the fashionable progressive public intellectuals of their time, the advice they tend to listen to is that offered by expensive pollsters, focus groups organizers and political strategists.

Quo vadis social democracy?

In its 160 or so years of history, social democracy has been one of the most influential ideologies and social movements of Europe. European social democrats campaigned and sacrificed themselves for the extension of suffrage to all men and women, devised forms of reforming and regulating capitalism, developed welfare states which contributed to the emancipation of workers and the protection of the most vulnerable and offered hope to those who believed that a more just world was possible. Even now, amid yet another existential crisis, social democracy is still one of the main political forces in European politics.

In light of its original goals, the track record of social democracy is mixed. There is no doubt that social democracy transformed European societies, particularly those in western Europe, and emancipated millions of workers, albeit in a capitalist society. Without the role performed by social democratic parties, activists and intellectuals, living conditions in Europe would be very different from what they are now. The European social model, which is predicated on democracy and universal suffrage, robust labour and social rights, welfare states and a mixed economy is a joint achievement of European social democrats, liberals and Christian democrats. In this context, it seems fair to conclude that social democracy has been a transformative ideology.

However, social democrats failed in their mission to overthrow or create the conditions for the withering way of capitalism, which was the requisite for the full emancipation of workers and the development of a socialist society united by bonds of fellowship and cooperation. Capitalism has managed to survive many nearly fatal crises and has re-emerged as the hegemonic economic system, thanks in part to the role social democrats played in keeping it alive. But this social democratic failing needs to be put into perspective. Creating the conditions for the withering away of capitalism is an incredibly challenging task. At the very least, achieving that goal requires the mobilization of social, political and economic forces that can offer a countervailing power to capitalism.

In 160 or so years of history, social democrats were never in a position to become a countervailing force to capitalism, let alone to be close to overthrowing it. When they were in power, they faced the opposition of capital, which was well represented in centre-right parties, parliaments, the law, media organizations and other powerful institutions. Moreover, improving the working conditions of workers implied compromises with capitalism. And when they were faced with the several crises of capitalism, they realized that these were the wrong moments to start a transition to a socialist society. As Kautsky noted (1988 [1918]: 97), "the destruction of capitalism is not Socialism" because workers would be the first victims of that achievement.[4]

However, if social democrats failed in the mission of developing a socialist and non-capitalist society, they nonetheless transformed the lives of the workers they represented. What is not clear now is whether social democratic parties still have the political will to remain the standard-bearers of the transformational social democratic creed.

At the time of writing, European social democracy is still disorientated and electorally too weak to make a difference. Most European countries are governed by centre-right or radical right parties. In the few cases where social democrats lead governments, they face powerful constraints. In Germany, the SPD-led government has faced opposition from its liberal coalition partner to its plans to reform the eurozone. The Free Democratic Party's opposition to significant reform of the eurozone governance rules is consequential. Without a reform of the governance rules of the monetary union it is not possible to develop social democratic policies in Europe. In Spain, the PSOE-led government has introduced important labour market reforms and offered sustained support to voters over the cost-of-living crisis, but these reforms have done little to slow down the fragmentation of the party system or to address the structural inequalities that divide Spanish society. In Portugal, the socialist government has raised wages and pensions and introduced social democratic measures such as universal free childcare, but the eurozone's deficit rules prevent it from investing in the public services and infrastructure that have the potential to transform the economy and reduce inequalities. In Denmark, the social democrats lead a coalition government but at the cost of adopting highly restrictive immigration policies which question social democratic support for human rights and internationalism. In short, these social democratic-led governments face challenging constraints at the domestic and international levels and are isolated at the EU level, which is now the arena where key decisions are taken for all areas of public policy.

For these reasons, this fourth act remains unfinished and open to possibilities. Of all the possible paths they can pursue, three stand out as plausible. Each of them is consequential for the future of social democracy. The first path, which reflects the current state of social democratic disorientation and powerlessness, involves developing political programmes that offer voters palliative remedies for the multiple crises Europe faces. These remedies may offer some immediate relief for the pain many voters face, but they will neither offer a cure for any of the many crises, nor will they lead to the development of a stable coalition of voters that will keep social democrats in power for a long time. Crucially, this path takes social democratic parties into new ideological territory as they will no longer be practising social democracy in any recognizable form. At best, social democratic parties will be practising a hybrid ideology which combines social liberalism, Christian democracy, the palest tinges of environmentalism and a rhetorical and vague commitment to the values and ends of social democracy. If that is their choice, the fourth act of social democracy will be its last.

The second path follows from the first and involves both exhaustion and renewal. Social democratic parties may well accept that social democracy has reached the end of the road. But this decision does not necessarily mean the end of social democracy. There are other political forces – namely the parties of the radical left and greens that, since the global financial crisis of 2008, have become the standard-bearers of the values and policies of postwar social democracy – that may decide to carry the torch of social democracy. In Greece, Syriza has become a de facto social democratic party, replacing PASOK as the main centre-left party. Similarly, the Greens and La France Insoumise offer a counterpoint to the French PS.

The third choice is more ambitious, and for that reason it is more difficult to put into practice. This third path involves rediscovering the social democratic commitment to transform society and proposing a programme of human emancipation for the twenty-first century. This programme will have to consider the impact of globalization over the capacity of the nation state to govern in a social democratic fashion and defend a reformed and regulated form of capitalism. This reckoning with globalization must defend the use of the market-making powers of the state to regulate global capitalism in a way that serves the public interest. Having accepted that, although constrained, the state is not a powerless agent, social democrats should focus their energies on deepening democracy, especially in the economic sphere (but without neglecting the political sphere), tackling the climate emergency and developing networks of solidarity within societies. Following this path will not be easy. Social democrats will face formidable opposition to their plans. In the current fragmented and polarized political landscape, they will have to build a truly international movement and find transnational and national allies that represent different but ideologically congenial traditions to turn this programme into a reality.

There are signs that some social democratic and centre-left politicians are keen to develop an ambitious and transformational agenda that seeks to turn the page on neoliberalism. In the United States, the Democratic president, Joe Biden, launched a range of initiatives (discussed briefly in Chapter 4) that seek to address the shortcomings of neoliberalism by proposing an economic approach that promotes prosperity for all and addresses the climate emergency. Biden's agenda is predicated on the development of national productive capacities (especially in the sectors which are key to the green transition) through an active and conditional industrial policy,[5] the introduction of labour and environmental protections on trade agreements, a more progressive tax system and investment in infrastructure. "Bidenomics" has partly influenced the economic agenda of the British Labour Party led by Keir Starmer. In the EU, the unprecedented Next Generation recovery plan, announced in 2020 and worth €750 billion, opened the vistas of European social democrats as the plan enables ambitious programmes of investment in infrastructure and skills and a transition to renewable energy, as well as substantial wealth transfers to the countries of the southern and eastern peripheries. Despite its ambitious scale, the EU's recovery plan leaves the eurozone governance rules unchanged.

But the limitations of the EU recovery plan should not be seen as insurmountable. After all, national governments decide the policy agenda of the EU. At the time of writing, most EU member states are led by centre-right or radical right governments. However, nothing stops social democratic-led governments from forging alliances with political forces that recognize the necessity of transformational change and pushing for more reforms. As this volume showed, many of the challenges faced by social democratic parties have resulted from their own choices and decisions, which in turn reflected their own interpretations of social democratic doctrines, as well as their own understanding of how to bring them to fruition in the concrete circumstances in which they found themselves. What this implies is that the main condition for the revival of European social democracy is a voluntaristic commitment to its ends and values. If social democrats renew their commitment to the goals and values of European social democracy, other acts will follow the fourth. But for the time being, in this moment of *interregnum*, the future of social democracy remains uncertain but open.

Notes

Introduction

1. There is a wealth of literature on the history and transformation of European social democracy. This volume has been influenced by a variety of insightful and original works listed in the Further Reading section at the back of the book.
2. Wolfgang Streeck and Kathleen Thelen define drift, layering, displacement and conversion in the following manner: *drift* involves the active neglect of an institution or practice and of nondecisions; *layering* involves the introduction of new elements to existing institutions; *displacement* happens as new models emerge which call into question previously taken-for-granted organizational forms and practices; a conversion is a process where institutions "are allowed to decay as they are *redirected to new goals, functions, or purposes*" (Streeck & Thelen 2010: 19–27).
3. The SPD resulted from the fusion of the General German Workers' Union led by Ferdinand Lassalle and of the Social Democratic Workers' Party, led by August Bebel and Wilhelm Liebknecht. Both parties had been created in the 1860s.

Chapter 1

1. In a speech to the Hague Congress of the Workingmen's International Association, Marx argued: "One day the working class must hold political power in its hands in order to establish a new organization of labour; it must overthrow the old political system which maintains the old institutions in being, unless it wishes, like the early Christians, who despised and neglected such action, to renounce 'the kingdom of this world'" (Marx 1934 [1864]: 165).
2. Marx's quote was: The working classes "have no ideals to realise, they only have to set at liberty the elements of the new society which have already been developed in the womb of the collapsing bourgeois society". Lenin was furious with Bernstein's use of Marx's quote. Without naming Bernstein, Lenin claimed that "it is an essential correction that has been distorted by the opportunists" (Lenin 1992 [1917]: 34).
3. At the height of the Dreyfus crisis in 1899, a government of Republican Defence was formed under Rene Waldeck-Rousseau. To the consternation of several French socialists, a leading independent socialist, Alexandre Millerand, joined the government as a minister of commerce. While in government, he secured

significant reforms, namely the reduction of the working week, the strengthening of the industrial inspectorate, the creation of labour councils and the use of public contracts to improve working conditions. But the symbolism of joining a government containing General Gaston Gallifet, the butcher of the 1871 Paris Commune, was intolerable for many Communards (Eley 2002: 87–8).

4. In 1914, when the SPD declared its support for the war, Lenin declared he was no longer a social democrat but a communist.

Chapter 2

1. The Spartacist League and the USPD merged in 1920.
2. Rudolf Hilferding had been a member of the USPD but, following the merger of the USPD with the Spartacist League, he joined the ranks of the SPD. He also acquired German citizenship in 1919.
3. The Stavisky affair was a financial scandal that compromised the Radical Socialists.
4. Keynesianism also challenged the idea that markets were self-regulating and argued instead that government intervention was required to stabilize the economy, especially during a recession. Keynesianism also rejected the idea that markets would automatically promote full employment. For that reason, Keynes argued that aggregate demand was the most important force driving the economy, especially during a recession.
5. The Bad Godesberg included a surprisingly radical approach to competition policy. In fact, the SPD sought to exempt public companies and cooperatives from the anti-cartel law. As Brian Shaev argued, the SPD's approach to competition policy aimed to develop tools to enable governments to coordinate macroeconomic programming that would steer national and international economies towards goals of general welfare (Shaev 2020).
6. As Andry explained, the original Vredeling directive required companies employing over 1,000 workers, of whom at least 150 were in two different countries, to negotiate and create a transnational body of workers' representatives, with legal rights to information and consultation. But the directive, which was adopted in 1994, established that the European Works Councils were not mandatory but negotiated after an initiative launched by at least 100 employees; the directive only covers general requirements for the European Works Council and promotes flexibility and encourages the promotion of a corporate culture which prioritises the interests of management (Andry 2022: 272).
7. Eurocommunism was pioneered by the PCI and defended a type of communism which dissociated itself from the Soviet Union and participated in parliamentary democracy. This movement became very popular in the 1970s and claimed that each communist party should base their policies on the needs and traditions of their own countries.

Chapter 3

1. Ordoliberalism is a German variant of neoliberalism which argues that the state plays a key role in the market economy, namely in the protection of economic competition. In economic terms, ordoliberal policies rely on following strict rules on public deficits, inflation and fiscal rectitude. More specifically, as Quinn Slobodian explained, ordoliberalism "is less a theory of the market or of economics than of law and the state" (Slobodian 2018: 269).
2. The convergence criteria of the European Monetary Union reflect ordoliberal values; see Blyth (2013: 138–41).
3. By neoliberal turn I mean a shift to the promotion of market values over other values. As William Davies explained, neoliberalism is not a unified doctrine. In fact, the term has inspired several schools: the Austrian school (also known as the Geneva School) associated with Friedrich Hayek and Ludwig von Mises, the German ordoliberal school associated with the Freiburg School and the Chicago school associated with Milton Friedman. But as Davies argues, there is a common thread uniting the different strands of neoliberalism, which is "an attempt to replace political judgement with economic evaluation, including, but not exclusively, the evaluations offered by markets" (Davies 2017: 5–6). As identified by international organizations such as the International Monetary Fund, neoliberalism has been associated with the policies of deregulation, privatization and liberalization. The purpose of this policy mix has been to, as Quinn Slobodian argued, design "institutions – not to liberate markets but to encase them, to inoculate capitalism against the threat of democracy, to create a framework to contain often irrational human behaviour, and to reorder the world after empire as a space of competing states in which borders fulfil a necessary function" (Slobodian 2018: 2). Florence Sutcliffe-Braithwaite, Aled Davies and Ben Jackson have also offered a neat definition of neoliberalism. As they put it, "neoliberals believed that the state should be repurposed and redeployed *to create and uphold* markets and competition" (Sutcliffe-Braithwaite *et al.* 2021: 3).
4. Quinn Slobodian argues that the Treaty of Rome (1957), which founded the European Economic Community, laid the foundations for the creation of an economic constitution which would prioritise the pursuit of economic competition through legal means over other economic, social or political goals (Slobodian 2018: 208–10).
5. These criteria ruled that participants in the single currency had to keep inflation at 1.5 per cent and public debt below 60 per cent of GDP, and that the public deficit should not exceed 3 per cent of GDP.
6. The new Clause Four stated Labour's belief in the principle of community "in which power, wealth and opportunity are in the hands of the many not the few".
7. In Britain, the modernization of public services introduced by New Labour followed what Eric Shaw defined as "New Labour managerialism", which was "grounded in a strong commitment to a large and vibrant sphere of collective activity where public goods such as a healthcare and schooling were provided in equitable fashion according to need, free at the point of delivery and funded by progressive taxation" but which "was convinced that the techniques and norms of the private sector and, in some cases, the use of commercial providers, should be harnessed to improve the delivery of public services" (Shaw 2009: 152).

8. In his speech to the 2005 Labour Party Annual Conference, Tony Blair said: "I hear people say we have to stop and debate globalization. You might as well debate whether autumn should follow summer." He also said: "The temptation is to use government to try to protect ourselves against the onslaught of globalisation by shutting it out – to think we protect a workforce by regulation, a company by government subsidy, an industry by tariffs. It doesn't work today."

9. This dilution was expressed in an acceptance of inequalities, which rose during New Labour' time in office, and in its refusal to adopt progressive taxation measures. Mark Wickham-Jones argues that New Labour was not neoliberal because it retained "significant commitments to tax and spend and to intervention in the economy, as well as to a redistributive impulse" (Wickham-Jones 2021: 249).

Chapter 4

1. In *The Entrepreneurial State*, Mazzucato argues that in the history of modern capitalism the state has not only fixed markets but it has also created and shaped markets through investment in nascent technologies where the private sector does not dare to invest initially because there is no guaranteed return.

2. By "new productivism" Rodrik means an approach to political economy which emphasizes the "dissemination of productive economic opportunities throughout all regions and all segments of the labour force". Unlike neoliberalism, "new productivism" gives governments and civil society a significant role in achieving that goal. In addition, this approach puts "less faith in markets, is suspicious of large corporations and emphasizes production and investment over finance and local communities over globalization. New productivism also departs f from the Keynesian welfare state by focussing less on redistribution, social transfers, and macroeconomic management and more on supply-side measures to create good jobs for everyone" (Rodrik 2022).

3. The rise of Sumar, a left-wing movement led by Yolanda Diaz, signals the decline of the radical left party Podemos. Parties such as Izquierda Unida, Compromís and Más País (which results from a secession from Podemos) have joined Sumar.

Conclusion

1. This is a reference to George Gissing's novel *New Grub Street*, where he described the daily struggles and hand-to-mouth existence of the new class of journalists, writers and scholars forced to earn a living by writing for the many new publications that emerged in the late nineteenth century (Gissing 2008).

2. Friedrich Engels claimed that the "fear of the revolution" was the Fabians' "fundamental principle" (1934 [1893]: 505).

3. In this letter Engels writes: "if one thing is certain is that our Party and the working class can only come to power under the form of the democratic republic. This is even the specific form for the dictatorship of the proletariat, as the great French revolution has already shown" (Engels 1934 [1891]: 486).

4. Karl Kautsky was very clear about this. He argued that: "The destruction of capitalism is not Socialism. Where capitalist production cannot be transformed at once into Socialist production, it must go on as before, otherwise the process of production will be interrupted, and that hardship for the masses will ensure which modern proletariat so much fears in the shape of modern unemployment" (Kautsky 1988 [1918]: 97).

5. Biden's Inflation Reduction Act (2022) offers subsidies for companies to invest in the green transition, but those subsidies have conditionalities attached. To receive those subsidies, private companies need to comply with labour standards and protect social and economic rights.

A chronology of European social democracy

1838   The People's Charter is launched in London, the Chartist movement is born in response to the failure of the 1832 Reform Act to broaden the vote beyond the gentry. They demand universal manhood suffrage, secret ballots and shorter working days.

1839   First Convention of the Chartist Movement meets in London.

1847   The Communist Correspondence Committee is formed.

1848   The Springtime of the Peoples – a revolutionary wave in Europe; publication of the *Communist Manifesto*; universal male suffrage is granted in France.

1863   Foundation of the General German Workers' Association, which later fused with another party to form Germany's SPD.

1864   Foundation of the International Working Men's Association (known as the First International) in London.

1867   Karl Marx publishes first volume of *Das Kapital*.

1869   Foundation of Germany's Social Democratic Workers' Party.

1870   Start of the Franco-Prussian war which finished in May of 1871 with France's defeat.

1871   The Paris Commune is declared in February and two months later is violently disassembled. The Paris Commune was a defining moment for the European socialist movement.

1871   The German Empire is founded and establishes male universal suffrage.

1874   Foundation of Portuguese Socialist Party.

1875   Foundation of Germany's SPD from the merger of General German Workers' Association (1863) and the Social Democratic Workers' Party; SPD's Gotha Programme is approved.

1878   Germany's Chancellor Otto von Bismarck proclaims the Anti-Socialist Laws.

1879   Foundation of Spain's PSOE and of France's Party Ouvrier Français.

1883   Death of Karl Marx.

1884   UK's Fabian Society and Social Democratic Federation founded.

1887   Foundation of Norway's Labour Party.

1888   Foundation of Switzerland's Social Democratic Party.

1889   First Meeting of the Second Socialist International in Paris.

1889   Foundation of social democratic parties in Austria, Sweden and Finland.

1891   SPD approves the Erfurt Programme.

1892   Foundation of Italy's Workers' Party.

1893   Foundation of the UK's Independent Labour Party (ILP).

1894   Foundation of Belgium's social democratic party.

1895   Death of Friedrich Engels.

1898   Eduard Bernstein starts to "revise" Marxist doctrines. The Millerand Affair in France in which a leading independent socialist joined the Republican Defence government as commerce minister.

1900   British trade unions, the ILP, the Social Democratic Federation and the Fabian Society launch the Labour Representation Committee.

1905   Jean Jaurès, Jules Guesde and Paul Lafargue launches the Section Française de L'International Socialiste.

1914   Jean Jaurès is assassinated. Start of the First World War.

1917   Bolshevik Revolution in Russia. Sweden's SAP joins a government for the first time.

1918   The UK establishes universal suffrage. Lenin changes the name of Russia's Social Democratic and Workers' Party to the All-Russian Communist Party. German SPD joins a coalition government with the liberals and the right.

1919   Lenin creates the Comintern, which assembles the world's communist parties.

1920   France's PCF is founded following a secession from SFIO at the Tours Congress.

1921   Amadeo Bordiga, Antonio Gramsci and their associates decide to secede from the PSI to create the Italian Communist Party. Sweden establishes universal suffrage.

1924   The UK's Labour Party leads its first government with Ramsay Macdonald as prime minister. The government collapses after ten months in office.

1929–31   Labour wins a majority for the first time in a UK general election, returning Ramsay Macdonald as prime minister, who appoints Margaret Bondfield as the first woman cabinet member as minister of labour.

1932   Sweden's SAP starts its long period leading governments.

1936   A Popular Front government is formed in France; John Maynard Keynes publishes *The General Theory of Employment, Interest and Money*. This work influenced economic policy in the postwar period and informed the programmes of social democratic parties.

1942   The Beveridge Report, entitled *Social Insurance and Allied Services*, was published in the UK and became an instant bestseller. It recommended the establishment of a comprehensive welfare state to fight the "five giants": idleness, ignorance, disease, squalor and want.

1945   The Labour Party led by Clement Attlee wins the UK's general election. At the Potsdam Summit, Harold Truman, Josef Stalin and Clement Attlee negotiate the terms of the end of the war; Europe is divided between West and East.

1951   The Swedish economists Rudolf Meidner and Gösta Rehn publish the report *The Trade Union Movement and Full Employment* which proposes a new economic and wage model for Sweden. These proposals lead to the foundation of what became known as the Rehn–Meidner model, which aimed to promote low inflation, full employment, high economic growth and income equality.

1956   Anthony Crosland publishes *The Future of Socialism*, which proposed a revision of socialist doctrines.

1959   The German SPD approves a new programme at the Bad Godesberg Congress, whereby the party substantially revised its socialist doctrines.

1966   Germany's SPD joins a government for the first time since the 1920s.

1968   Mass student protests in Paris and other European cities symbolize the beginning of an era of social unrest in Europe.

1971   The SFIO is dismantled and in its place the PSF is founded.

1974   Democracy is re-established in Greece and established in Portugal.

1975   Willy Brandt, Bruno Kreisky and Olof Palme publish *Social Democracy and the Future* in an attempt to renew social democracy.

1976   Sweden's SAP loses its first election since 1932.

1978   Spain approves its democratic constitution.

1981   François Mitterrand is elected French president, the first left-wing politician to be elected to the post in France's Fifth Republic.

1981   PASOK wins Greece's general election.

1981   Sweden's SAP launches a Third Way programme.

1982   Felipe Gonzalez is elected Spain's first socialist prime minister, a post he occupies until 1996.

1983   Mitterrand announces the *tournant de la rigueur* and abandons the socialist programme he had promised at the 1981 presidential election.

1983	Italy elects Bettino Craxi as its first socialist prime minister.
1986	Swedish prime minister and social democratic leader Olof Palme is assassinated in Stockholm.
1990	Former Italian communists launch the PDS. The PSI is eclipsed as a result.
1994	Tony Blair is elected leader of the UK's Labour Party.
1996	Spain's PSOE loses election and remains in opposition until 2004.
1995	Portugal's PS returns to power after ten years in opposition.
1995	The Labour Party revises Clause Four of its constitution, which called for the common ownership of industry.
1997	Britain's Labour Party win the general election by a landslide with a majority of 179 seats. This was Labour's first electoral victory at a general election since 1974.
1997	The PSF leads a government of the Plural Left together with the Communist Party, the Greens, the Citizens' Movement and the Left's Radical Party.
1997	Coalition of left-wing parties *L'Ulivo* wins the Italian legislative elections.
1998	Germany's SPD wins the legislative elections; Gerhard Schröder becomes chancellor of an SPD–Green coalition.
1998	Tony Blair publishes the pamphlet *The Third Way: New Politics for the New Century*.
1998	Tony Blair and Gerhard Schroeder publish pamphlet *The Third Way/Neue Mitte*.
2001	Social democratic parties in Europe start to lose elections. This is the moment when the Third Way wave starts to unravel in Europe.
2006	Sweden's SAP obtains its worst results ever at a legislative election winning only 34.99 per cent share of the vote.
2010	The UK's Labour Party under the leadership of Gordon Brown loses its first elections since 1997; Greece obtained the first of three financial rescue package from the EU and IMF.
2011	Ireland and Portugal obtain a financial rescue package from the EU and IMF as a result of the eurozone crisis
2015	Danish social democrats lose elections.
2015	Portugal's Socialist Party leads a quasi-coalition government with three parties of the radical left.
2016	British citizens vote to leave the European Union in a national referendum on 23 June.

2017 French socialists suffer humiliating defeat at the presidential and legislative elections. The presidential candidate Benoit Hamon scores only 6.2 per cent at the election and the party obtains only 3.1 per cent share of the vote at the legislative elections.

2018 The PSOE led by Pedro Sánchez and Sweden's SAP return to power. "Yellow vests" protests start in France.

2019 Denmark's Social Democratic Party return to power after a legislative term in opposition.

2021 Germany's SPD wins the election and forms a coalition government with the Greens and the Liberal Party.

2022 Portugal's PS wins the second landslide victory in its history.

2022 Sweden's SAP loses legislative elections.

Further reading

Berman, S. 2006. *The Primacy of Politics: Social Democracy and the Making of Europe's Twentieth Century.* Cambridge: Cambridge University Press

Eley, G. 2002. *Forging Democracy: The History of the Left in Europe, 1850–2000.* Oxford: Oxford University Press.

Esping-Andersen, G. 1988. *Politics against Markets: The Social Democratic Road to Power.* Princeton, NJ: Princeton University Press.

Keman, H. 2017. *Social Democracy: A Comparative Account of the Left-Wing Party Family.* Abingdon: Routledge.

Lindemann, A. 1983. *A History of European Socialism.* Princeton, NJ: Princeton University Press.

Moschonas, G. 2002. *In the Name of Social Democracy: The Great Transformation – 1945 to the Present.* London: Verso.

Mudge, S. 2018. *Leftism Reinvented: Western Parties from Socialism to Neoliberalism.* Cambridge, MA: Harvard University Press.

Padgett, S. & W. Paterson 1991. *A History of Social Democracy in Postwar Europe.* Harlow: Longman.

Przeworski, A. 1993. *Capitalism and Social Democracy.* Cambridge: Cambridge University Press.

Przeworski, A. & J. Sprague 1986. *Paper Stones: A History of Electoral Socialism.* Chicago: University of Chicago Press

Sassoon, D. 1997. *One Hundred Years of Socialism: The West European Left in the Twentieth Century.* London: Fontana.

Smaldone, W. 2020. *European Socialism: A Concise History with Documents,* 2nd edition. London: Rowman & Littlefield.

Wright, T. 1996. *Socialisms: Old and New.* Abingdon: Routledge.

References

Abou-Chadi, T. & M. Wagner 2019. "The electoral appeal of party strategies in post-industrial societies: when can the mainstream left succeed?". *Journal of Politics* 81(4): 1405–20, https://www.zora.uzh.ch/id/eprint/178898/2/ZORA178898_1.pdf.

Abou-Chadi, T., R. Mitteregger & C. Mudde 2021. *Left behind by the Working Class? Social Democracy's Electoral Crisis and the Rise of the Radical Right*. Friedrich Ebert Foundation, https://library.fes.de/pdf-files/a-p-b/18074.pdf.

Adler, M. 2017 [1926]. "Towards a discussion of the New Party programme". In *Austro-Marxism: The Ideology of Unity*, Vol. 2, *Changing the World: The Politics of Austro-Marxism*, edited by M. Blum & W. Smaldone. Leiden: Brill.

Ágh, A. 2004. *The Europeanization of Social Democracy in East Central Europe*. Berlin: FES, https://library.fes.de/pdf-files/id/01971.pdf.

Åmark, K. 1992. "Social democracy and the trade union movement: solidarity and the politics of self-interest". In *Creating Social Democracy: A Century of the Social Democratic Labor Party in Sweden*, edited by K. Migeld, K. Molin & K. Åmark. University Park: Pennsylvania State University Press.

Amarnath, S., M. Brusseler, D. Gabor, L. Chirag & J. Mason 2023. "Varieties of derisking". *Phenomenal World*, 17 June, https://www.phenomenalworld.org/interviews/derisking/.

Andersson, J. 2016. "Losing social democracy: reflections on the erosion of a paradigmatic case of social democracy". In *European Social Democracy during the Global Economic Crisis: Renovation or Resignation?*, edited by D. Bayley, J.-M. de Waele, F. Escalona & M. Vieira. Manchester: Manchester University Press.

Andry, A. 2022. *Social Europe: The Road Not Taken – The Left and European Integration in the Long 1970s*. Oxford: Oxford University Press.

Atkinson, A. 2015. *Inequality: What Can Be Done?* Cambridge, MA: Harvard University Press.

Aviv, A. & I. Aviva 1981. "The Madrid working class, the Spanish Socialist Party and the collapse of the Second Republic (1934–1936)". *Journal of Contemporary History* 16(2): 229–50.

Azmanova, A. 2020. *Capitalism on Edge: How Fighting Precarity Can Achieve Radical Change without Crisis or Utopia*. New York: Columbia University Press.Bandau, F. 2022. "The electoral crisis of social democracy: postindustrial dilemmas or neoliberal contamination?". *Political Studies Review* 20(3): 493–503.

Bartolini, S. 2007. *The Political Mobilisation of the European Left, 1968–1980*. Cambridge: Cambridge University Press.

Bauer, O. 2017 [1909]. "The road to power". In *Austro-Marxism: The Ideology of Unity*, Vol. 2, *Changing the World: The Politics of Austro-Marxism*, edited by M. Blum & W. Smaldone. Leiden: Brill.

Bayley, D., J.-M. de Waele, F. Escalona & M. Vieira 2016. "Introduction". In *European Social Democracy during the Global Economic Crisis: Renovation or Resignation?*, edited by D. Bayley, J.-M. de Waele, F. Escalona & M. Vieira. Manchester: Manchester University Press.

Benedetto, G., S. Hix & N. Mastrorocco 2020. "The rise and fall of social democracy, 1917–2017". *American Political Science Review* 114(3): 928–39.

Bergström, V. 1992. "Party program and economic policy". In *Creating Social Democracy: A Century of the Social Democratic Labor Party in Sweden*, edited by K. Misgeld, K. Molin & K. Åmark, 131–73. University Park: Pennsylvania State University Press.

Berman, S. & M. Snegovaya 2019. "Populism and the decline of social democracy". *Journal of Democracy* 30(3): 5–19.

Berman, S. 2006. *The Primacy of Politics: Social Democracy and the Making of Europe's Twentieth Century*. Cambridge: Cambridge University Press.

Bernstein, E. 2021 [1899]. *Evolutionary Socialism*. Dickinson, ND: SAI Press.

Bernstein, E. 2004 [1899]. *The Preconditions of Socialism*, edited by Henry Tudor. Cambridge: Cambridge University Press.

Blair, T. & G. Schröder 1998. *The Third Way/Neue Mitte*. London/Berlin: Fabian Society/ Friedrich Ebert Stiftung, https://library.fes.de/pdf-files/bueros/suedafrika/02828. pdf.

Blair, T. 1996. "The global economy". Speech to the Keindanren, Tokyo, 5 January.

Blum, L. 2016 [1920]. "Discours de Léon Blum 27 Décembre 1920 – Congrès de Tours, 25–30 Décembre 1920". In *Léon Blum: Le Socialisme et la République*, edited by A. Bergounioux. Paris: Foundation Jean Jaurès/FEPS.

Blum, L. 2016 [1946]. "Discours de Léon Blum, 29 Août 1946, 38 Congrès National de la SFIO – 29 août–1 septembre". In *Léon Blum: Le Socialisme et la République*, edited by A. Bergounioux. Paris: Foundation Jean Jaurès/FEPS.

Blyth, M. 2013. *Austerity: The History of a Dangerous Idea*. Oxford: Oxford University Press.

Bouillard, C. 2016. "The French Socialist Party (2008–13): not revolutionaries, not luminaries, just 'normal' guys' amidst the tempest". In *European Social Democracy during the Global Economic Crisis: Renovation or Resignation?*, edited by D. Bayley, J.-M. de Waele, F. Escalona & M. Vieira, 153–75. Manchester: Manchester University Press.

Brandt, W., B. Kreisly & O. Palme 1976. *La Social-Démocratie et L'Avenir*. Paris: Gallimard.

Bremer, B. & L. Rennwald 2022. "Who still likes social democracy? The support base of social democratic parties reconsidered". *Party Politics* 24(4): 1–14.

Busch, A. & P. Manow 2001. "The SPD and the Neue Mitte in Germany". In *New Labour: The Progressive Future?*, edited by S. White. Basingstoke: Palgrave Macmillan.

Callaghan, J. 1976. "Leader's speech – Blackpool 1976", http://www.britishpoliticalspeech. org/speech-archive.htm?speech=174.

Camerra-Rowe, P. 2004. "Agenda 2010: redefining German social democracy". *German Politics & Society* 22(1): 1–30.

Chandler, D. 2023. *Free and Equal: What Would a Fair Society Look Like?* London: Allen Lane.

Cliffe, J. 2023. "Spain's left coalition defied expectation: can its leader, Pedro Sánchez, win again?" *New Statesman*, 19 April, https://www.newstatesman.com/world/europe/2023/04/spain-coalition-leader-pedro-sanchez.

Clift, B. 2009. "The political economy of French social democratic economic policy autonomy 1997–2002: credibility, dirigisme and globalisation". In *In Search of Social Democracy*, edited by J. Callaghan, N. Fishman, B. Jackson & M. McIvor. Manchester: Manchester University Press.

Colton, J. 1953. "Léon Blum and the French Socialists as a government party". *Journal of Politics* 15(4): 517–43.

Crosland, A. 2006 [1956]. *The Future of Socialism*. London: Constable.

Dahrendorf, R. 1980. *After Social Democracy*. London: Liberal Publication Department.

Davies, W. 2017. *The Limits of Neoliberalism: Authority, Sovereignty and the Logic of Competition*, revised edition. London: Sage.

De Deken, J. 1999. "The German Social Democratic Party". In *Social Democratic Parties in the European Union: History, Organization and Policies*, edited by R. Ladrech & P. Marlière, 79–94. Basingstoke: Palgrave Macmillan.

De Man, H. 1927. *The Psychology of Socialism*. London: Holt.

Di Donato, M. 2015. "The Cold War and socialist identity: the Socialist International and the 'Italian Communist Question' in the 1970s". *Contemporary European History* 24(2): 193–211.

Diamond, P. 2021. *The British Labour Party in Opposition and Power 1979–2019: Forward March Halted?* Abingdon: Routledge.

Diamond, P. 2023. "The resistible corrosion of Europe's center-left: the case of the British Labour Party since the 2008 financial crisis". In *The Resistible Corrosion of Europe's Center-Left After 2008*, edited by G. Menz. Abingdon: Routledge.

Dimitrakopoulos, D. & A. Passas 2011. "The panhellenic socialist movement and European integration: the primacy of the leader". In *Social Democracy and European Integration*, edited by D. Dimitrakopoulos. Abingdon: Routledge.

Eatwell, R. & M. Goodwin 2018. *National Populism: The Revolt against Liberal Democracy*. London: Penguin.

Eckhardt, W. 2016. *The First Socialist Schism: Bakunin vs Marx in the International Working Men's Association*. Oakland, CA: PM Press.

Eley, G. 2002. *Forging Democracy: The History of the Left in Europe, 1850–2000*. Oxford: Oxford University Press.

Engels, F. 1934 [1872]. "Letter to Theodor Cuno, 24 January 1872". In *Karl Marx and Friedrich Engels Correspondence 1846–1895*, edited by D. Torr. London: Martin Lawrence.

Engels, F. 1934 [1875]. "Letter to Bebel, 18–19 March 1875". In *Karl Marx and Friedrich Engels Correspondence 1846–1895*, edited by D. Torr. London: Martin Lawrence.

Engels, F. 1934 [1891]. "Letter to Kautsky, 29 June 1891". In *Karl Marx and Friedrich Engels Correspondence 1846–1895*, edited by D. Torr. London: Martin Lawrence.

Engels, F. 1934 [1893]. "Letter to Sorge, 18 January 1983". In *Karl Marx and Friedrich Engels Correspondence 1846–1895*, edited by D. Torr. London: Martin Lawrence.

Engels, F. 1969 [1880]. "Socialism: utopian and scientific". In *Karl Marx and Friedrich Engels: Basic Writings on Politics and Philosophy*, edited by L. Feuer. Glasgow: Fontana.

Engels, F. 1978 [1895]. "The tactics of social democracy – 1895". In *The Marx-Engels Reader*, second edition, edited by R. Tucker. New York: Norton.

Engels, F. 1998 [1888]. "Preface to English edition". In *The Communist Manifesto*, K. Marx & F. Engels. Oxford: Oxford University Press.Escalona, F. & M. Vieira 2016. "'It does not happen here either': why social democrats fail in the context of the Great Economic Crisis". In *European Social Democracy during the Global Economic Crisis: Renovation or Resignation?*, edited by D. Bayley, J.-M. de Waele, F. Escalona & M. Vieira. Manchester: Manchester University Press.

Esping-Andersen, G. 1985. *Politics against Markets: The Social Democratic Road to Power*. Princeton, NJ: Princeton University Press.

Esping-Andersen, G. 1992. "The making of a social democratic welfare state". In *Creating Social Democracy: A Century of the Social Democratic Labor Party in Sweden*, edited by K. Misgeld, K. Molin & K. Åmark, 35–66. University Park: Pennsylvania State University Press.

Evans, G. & A. Menon 2017. *Brexit and British Politics*. Cambridge: Polity.

Fagerholm, A. 2013. "Towards a lighter shade of red? Social democratic parties and the rise of neoliberalism in western Europe, 1970–1999". *Perspectives in European Politics and Society* 14(4): 538–61.

Fraser, N. 2019. *The Old Is Dying and the New Cannot Be Born*. London: Verso.

Fredriksen, K. 2012. "Income inequality in the European Union". OECD Economics Department Working Papers No. 952, 16 April, https://read.oecd-ilibrary.org/economics/income-inequality-in-the-european-union_5k9bdt47q5zt-en#page1.

Freeden, M. 1998. *Ideologies and Political Theory: A Conceptual Approach*. Oxford: Clarendon Press.

Gamble, A. 2009. *The Spectre at the Feast: Capitalist Crisis and the Politics of Recession*. Basingstoke: Palgrave Macmillan.

Ganz, J. 2023. "Have you heard of the 'polycrisis', yet?". *Unpopular Front*, 10 February, https://johnganz.substack.com/p/have-you-heard-about-the-polycrisis.

Giddens, A. 1994. *Beyond Left and Right: The Future of Radical Politics*. Cambridge: Polity.

Giddens, A. 1998. *The Third Way: The Renewal of Social Democracy*. Cambridge: Polity.

Gissing, G. 2008. *New Grub Street*. Oxford: Oxford University Press.

Goes, E. 2016. *The Labour Party under Ed Miliband: Trying but Failing to Renew Social Democracy*. Manchester: Manchester University Press.

Goes, E. 2018. "'Jez we can' Labour's campaign: a defeat with a taste of victory". *Parliamentary Affairs* 71 (Suppl. issue): 59–71.

Goes, E. 2020. "Labour's campaign: a defeat of epic proportions". *Parliamentary Affairs* 73 (Suppl. issue): 84–102.

Gould, P. 1998. *The Unfinished Revolution: How the Modernisers Saved the Labour Party*. London: Little Brown.

Green-Pedersen, C. & K. van Kersbergen 2002. "The politics of the Third Way: the transformation of social democracy in Denmark and the Netherlands". *Party Politics* 8(5): 507–24.

Grossman, E. & N. Mayer 2022. "A new form of anti-government resentment? Making sense of mass support for the Yellow-Vest movement in France". *Journal of Elections, Public Opinion & Parties* 22(November): 1–23.

Guger, A. 2001. "The Austrian experience". In *Social Democracy in Neoliberal Times: The Left and Economic Policy since 1980*, edited by A. Glyn. Oxford: Oxford University Press.

Guttsmann, W. 1981. *The German Social Democratic Party, 1875–1933: From Ghetto to Government*. London: Allen & Unwin.

Hall, P. & R. Taylor 1996. "Political science and the three new institutionalisms". *Political Studies* 44(5): 936–57.

Hertner, I. 2018. *Centre-Left Parties and the European Union: Power, Accountability, and Democracy.* Manchester: Manchester University Press.

Häusermann, S., H. Kitschelt, T. Abou-Chadi, M. Ares, D. Bischof, T. Kurer, M. van Ditmars & M. Wagner 2021. *Transformation of the Left: The Myth of Voter Losses to the Radical Right.* Friedrich Ebert Stiftung, January, https://library.fes.de/pdf-files/id/ipa/17385.pdf.

Hilferding, R. 2017 [1920]. "Revolutionary politics or illusions of power?", in *Austro-Marxism: The Ideology of Unity*, Vol. 2, *Changing the World: The Politics of Austro-Marxism*, edited by M. Blum & W. Smaldone. Leiden: Brill.

Hilferding, R. 2017 [1927]. "The task of social democracy in the Republic". In *Austro-Marxism: The Ideology of Unity*, Vol. 2, *Changing the World: The Politics of Austro-Marxism*, edited by M. Blum & W. Smaldone. Leiden: Brill.

Hilferding, R. 2017 [1930]. "In the danger zone". In *Austro-Marxism: The Ideology of Unity*, Vol. 2, *Changing the World: The Politics of Austro-Marxism*, edited by M. Blum & W. Smaldone. Leiden: Brill.

Hobsbawm, E. 1994. *The Age of Extremes: The Short Twentieth Century 1914–1991.* London: Michael Joseph.

Hobsbawm, E. 1995a. *The Age of Capital: 1848–1875.* London: Weidenfeld & Nicolson.

Hobsbawm, E. 1995b. *The Age of Empire: 1875–1914.* London: Weidenfeld & Nicolson.

Holmes, M. 2019. "Frankfurt's way or Labour's way: the Irish left and the crisis". In *The European Left and the Financial Crisis*, edited by M. Holmes & K. Order. Manchester: Manchester University Press.

Holmes, M. & S. Lightfoot 2011. "Limited influence? The role of the party of European Socialists in shaping social democracy in Central and Eastern Europe". *Government and Opposition* 46(1): 32–55.

Holmes, M. & S. Lightfoot 2016. "Limits of consensus? The party of European socialists and the financial crisis", in *European Social Democracy During the Global Financial Crisis: Renovation or Resignation?*, edited by D. Bayley, J.-M. de Waele, F. Escalona and P. Vieira. Manchester: Manchester University Press.

Holmes, M. & K. Roder 2019. "The European left and the crisis: opportunity or catastrophe?". In *The European Left and the Financial Crisis*, edited by M. Holmes & K. Order. Manchester: Manchester University Press.

Jaurès, J. 2015 [1901]. *Études Socialistes: Essai.* Amazon Digital Services LLC-KDP.

Jaurès, J. 2021 [1899]. "The socialism of the French Revolution, 22 October 1890". In *Selected Writings of Jean Jaurès*, edited by J.-N. Ducange & E. Marcobelli. Cham, Switzerland: Palgrave Macmillan.

Jaurès, J. 2022 [1908]. *A Socialist History of the French Revolution.* London: Pluto.

Judt, T. 1976. "The French Socialist and the Cartel des Gauches of 1924", *Journal of Contemporary History* 11: 199–215.

Judt, T. 2007. *Postwar: A History of Europe Since 1945.* London: Pimlico.

Jun, U. 2018. "Germany: little hope in times of crisis". In *Why the Left Loses: The Decline of the Centre-Left in Comparative Perspective*, edited by R. Manwaring & P. Kennedy. Bristol: Policy Press.

Karreth, J., J. Polk & C. Allen 2012. "Catchall or catch and release? The electoral consequences of social democratic parties' march to the middle in Western Europe". *Comparative Political Studies* 46(7): 791–822.

Kautsky, K. 1903. *The Social Revolution*. London: Charles Kerr.

Kautsky, K. 1988 [1918]. "Socialist democracy". In *Marxism: Essential Writings*, edited by D. McLellan. Oxford, Oxford University Press.

Kautsky, K. 2003 [1909]. *The Road to Power*. Germany: Block.

Kautsky, K. 2017 [1920]. "The development of a Marxist". *Historical Materialism* 25(3): 148–90.

Kautsky, K. 2021 [1892]. *The Class Struggle: Erfurt Program*. Milton Keynes: Ingram.

Keman, H. 2017. *Social Democracy: A Comparative Account of the Left-Wing Party Family*. Abingdon: Routledge.

Keman, H. 2023. "The continued decline of Dutch social democracy". In *The Resistible Corrosion of Europe's Centre-Left After 2008*, edited by G. Menz. Abingdon: Routledge.

Kennedy, P. 2016. "Back to the drawing board: the PSOE after the 2011 general election". In *European Social Democracy during the Global Economic Crisis: Renovation or Resignation?*, edited by D. Bayley, J.-M. de Waele, F. Escalona & M. Vieira, 176–92. Manchester: Manchester University Press.

Kennedy, P. 2009. "The Spanish Socialist Workers' Party: continuity, innovation and renewal". In *In Search of Social Democracy*, edited by J. Callaghan, N. Fishman, B. Jackson & M. McIvor. Manchester: Manchester University Press.

Kitschelt, H. 1993. "Class structure and social democratic party strategy". *British Journal of Political Science* 23(3): 299–337.

Kitschelt, H. 1994. *The Transformation of European Social Democracy*. Cambridge: Cambridge University Press.

Kitschelt, H. & S. Häusermann 2021. *Transformation of the Left: Strategic Options for Social Democratic Parties*. Berlin: Friedrich Ebert Foundation, https://library.fes.de/pdf-files/id/ipa/17383.pdf.

Klemperer, D. 2022. "The strange death of socialist France". *Renewal: A Journal of Social Democracy* 30(3): 43–53.

Ladrech, R. 1999. "Postscript: social democratic parties and the European Union". In *Social Democratic Parties in the European Union*, edited by R. Ladrech & P. Marlière. Basingstoke: Palgrave Macmillan.

Lane, D. 2021. "V. I. Lenin's theory of socialist revolution". *Critical Sociology* 47(3): 455–73.

LaPalombara, J. 1982. "Socialist alternatives: the Italian variant". *Foreign Affairs* 60(4): 924–42.

Laybourn, K. 2013. "The fall of the first MacDonald government, 1924". In *How Labour Governments Fall: From Ramsay MacDonald to Gordon Brown*, edited by T. Heppell & K. Theakston. Basingstoke: Palgrave Macmillan.

Lenin, V. 1992 [1917]. *The State and Revolution*. London: Penguin.

Leser, N. 1976. "Austro-Marxism: a reappraisal". *Journal of Contemporary History* 11(2/3): 133–48.

Lindemann, A. 1983. *A History of European Socialism*. Princeton, NJ: Princeton University Press.

Lipset, S. 1983. "Radicalism or reformism: the sources of working-class politics". *American Political Science Review* 77(1): 1–18.

Lordon, F. 2015. "The left and the euro: liquidate, rebuild". Verso blog, 25 July, https://www.versobooks.com/blogs/2150-the-left-and-the-euro-liquidate-rebuild.

Lordon, F. 2001. "The logic and limits of *désinflation compétitive*". In *Social Democracy in Neoliberal Times: The Left and Economic Policy since 1980*, edited by A. Glyn. Oxford: Oxford University Press.

Loxbo, K., J. Hinnfors, M. Hagevi, S. Bombäck & M. Demker 2019. "The decline of western European social democracy: exploring the transformed link between welfare state generosity and the electoral strength of social democratic parties, 1975–2014". *Party Politics* 27(3): 1–12.

Luxembourg, R. 2021. *Reform or Revolution and Other Writings*. New York: Dover.

Manwaring, R. 2021. *The Politics of Social Democracy: Issues, Dilemmas and Future Directions for the Centre-Left*. Abingdon: Routledge.

Manwaring, R. & P. Kennedy 2018. "Why the left loses: understanding the comparative decline of the centre-left". In *Why the Left Loses: The Decline of the Centre-Left in Comparative Perspective*, edited by R. Manwaring & P. Kennedy. Bristol: Policy Press.

Marks, G., H. Mbaye & H. Kim 2009. "Radicalism or reformism? Socialist parties before World War One". *American Sociology Review* 74(4): 615–35.

Martín, J. 2019. "The Italian left and the crisis: the case of Matteo Renzi's Partito Democratico". In *The European Left and the Financial Crisis*, edited by M. Holmes & K. Roder. Manchester: Manchester University Press.

Martell, L. 2012. "Social democracy in a global era". In *After the Third Way: The Future of Social Democracy in Europe*, edited by O. Cramme & P. Diamond. London: I. B. Tauris.

Marx, K. 1864. "Inaugural Address of the International Working Men's Association", 21–24 October, https://www.marxists.org/archive/marx/works/1864/10/27.htm.

Marx, K. 1934 [1864]. "Letter to Engels, 4 November 1864". In *Karl Marx and Friedrich Engels Correspondence 1846–1895*, edited by D. Torr. London: Martin Lawrence.

Marx, K. 1978. "After the Revolution: Marx Debates Bakunin". In *The Marx-Engels Reader*, edited by R. Tucker. New York: Norton.

Marx, K. 1996 [1852]. "The Eighteenth Brumaire of Louis Bonaparte". In *Marx: Later Political Writings*, edited and translated by T. Carver. Cambridge: Cambridge University Press.

Marx, K. 1996 [1871]. "The civil war in France: address of the General Council of the International Working-Men's Association to all members of the Association in Europe and the United States". In *Marx: Later Political Writings*, edited and translated by T. Carver. Cambridge: Cambridge University Press.

Marx, K. 1996 [1875]. "Critique of the Gotha Programme: marginal notes on the programme of the German Worker's Party". In *Marx: Later Political Writings*, edited and translated by T. Carver. Cambridge: Cambridge University Press.

Marx, K. & F. Engels 1934 [1879] "Letter to Bebel, Liebknecht, Bracke and Others", in *Karl Marx and Friedrich Engels Correspondence 1846-1895*, edited by B. Torr. London: Martin Lawrence.Marx, K. & F. Engels 1998 [1848]. *The Communist Manifesto*. Oxford: Oxford University Press.

Mazzucato, M. 2013. *The Entrepreneurial State: Debunking Public vs Private Sector Myths*. London: Anthem.

McKibbin, R. 1984. "Why was there no Marxism in Great Britain?" *English Historical Review* 99(391): 297–331.

McLellan, D. 1998. "Introduction". In *The Communist Manifesto* by K. Marx & F. Engels. Oxford: Oxford University Press.

McLellan, D. 2007. *Marxism after Marx*. Basingstoke: Palgrave Macmillan.

Menz, G. 2023. "The not so inevitable decline of social democracy in Germany". In *The Resistible Corrosion of Europe's Center-Left after 2008*, edited by G. Menz. Abingdon: Routledge.

Merkel, W. 1989. "After the golden age: a decline of social democratic policies in Western Europe during the 1980s?" CES Working Paper No. 20, Harvard University, https://ideas.repec.org/p/zbw/esrepo/112689.html.

Michels, R. 1966 [1911]. *Political Parties: A Sociological Study of the Oligarchical Tendencies of Modern Democracy*, 2nd paperback edition. New York: Free Press.

Mitchell, W. & T. Fazi 2017. *Reclaiming the State: A Progressive Vision of Sovereignty for a post-Neoliberal World*. London: Pluto.

Molin, K. 1992. "Historical orientation". In *Creating Social Democracy: A Century of the Social Democratic Labor Party in Sweden*, edited by K. Misgeld, K. Molin & K. Åmark. University Park: Pennsylvania State University Press.

Montebello, R., J. Spiteri & P. Von Brockdorff 2022. "Trade unions and income inequality: evidence from a panel of European countries". *International Labour Review*, https://doi.org/10.1111/ilr.12373.

Moschonas, G. 2009. "Reformism in a 'conservative' system: the European Union and social democratic identity". In *In Search of Social Democracy*, edited by J. Callaghan, N. Fishman, B. Jackson & M. McIvor. Manchester: Manchester University Press.

Moschonas, G. 2002. *In the Name of Social Democracy: The Great Transformation – 1945 to the Present*. London: Verso.

Moschonas, G. 1998. "Social-Démocratie et Électorat Ouvrier le Relâchement du Lien Social". *Actuel Marx* 23, L'Arbre Social-Démocrate, 93–115.

Motos, C. 2019. "The changing nature of the Spanish left: an uncertain balance". In *The European Left and the Financial Crisis*, edited by M. Holmes & K. Roder. Manchester: Manchester University Press.

Mudge, S. 2015. "Explaining political tunnel vision". *European Journal of Sociology* 56(1): 63–91.

Mudge, S. 2018. *Leftism Reinvented: Western Parties from Socialism to Neoliberalism*. Cambridge, MA: Harvard University Press.

Nedergaard, P. 2023. "Bucking the trend: the extraordinary bounce back of the Danish centre-left". In *The Resistible Corrosion of Europe's Centre-Left after 2008*, edited by G. Menz. Abingdon: Routledge.

O'Neill, M. & T. Williamson 2014. "Introduction". In *Property-Owning Democracy: Rawls and beyond*, edited by M. O'Neill & T. Williamson. Chichester: Wiley-Blackwell.

Oskarson, M. 2021. "Sweden's Social Democrats turn left". *IPS Journal*, 13 December, https://www.ips-journal.eu/topics/future-of-social-democracy/swedens-social-democrats-turn-left-5605/.

Oskarson, M. 2023. "The slow but persistent erosion of the Swedish Social Democratic Party". In *The Resistible Corrosion of Europe's Centre-Left after 2008*, edited by G. Menz. Abingdon: Routledge.

Oudenampsen, M. 2021. "The riddle of the missing feathers: rise and decline of the Dutch Third Way". *European Politics and Society* 22(1): 38–52.

Padgett, S. & W. Paterson 1991a. *A History of Social Democracy in Postwar Europe*. Harlow: Longman.

Padgett, S. & W. Paterson 1991b. "The rise and fall of the West German left". *New Left Review* 1/186 (April).

Paterson, W. & J. Sloam 2006. "Is the left alright? The SPD and the renewal of European social democracy". *German Politics* 15(3): 233–48.

Pautz, H. 2009. "The modernisation of German social democracy: towards a German Third Way and back". In *In Search of Social Democracy*, edited by J. Callaghan, N. Fishman, B. Jackson & M. McIvor. Manchester: Manchester University Press.

Pels, D. 1987. "Hendrik de Man and the ideology of planism". *International Review of Social History* 32(3): 206–29.

PES 2014. *PES Manifesto: Towards a New Europe*. Brussels: Party of European Socialists, https://publications.pes.eu/wp-content/uploads/2023/02/PES30Book_WEB_Bookmarked-reduced.pdf#page=143.

Pierson, P. 2000. "Increasing returns, path dependence, and the study of politics". *American Political Science Review* 94(2): 251–67.

Piketty, T. 2014. *Capital in the Twenty-First Century*. Cambridge, MA: Harvard University Press.

Piketty, T. 2020. *Capital and Ideology*. Cambridge, MA: Harvard University Press.

Polacko, M. 2022. "The rightward shift and electoral decline of social democratic parties under increasing inequality". *West European Politics* 45(4): 665–92.

Pontusson, J. 1995. "Explaining the decline of European social democracy: the role of structural economic change". *World Politics* 47(4): 495–533.

Przeworski, A. 1993. *Capitalism and Social Democracy*. Cambridge: Cambridge University Press.

Przeworski, A. 2001. "How many ways can be third?" In *Social Democracy in Neoliberal Times: The Left and Economic Policy Since 1980*, edited by A. Glyn. Oxford: Oxford University Press.

Przeworski, A. & J. Sprague 1986. *Paper Stones: A History of Electoral Socialism*. Chicago: University of Chicago Press.

Racz, B. 1993. "The socialist-left opposition in post-communist Hungary". *Europe-Asia Studies* 45(4): 647–70.

Ramos, C. 2019. "Gerigonça: the Portuguese left approach to the crisis". In *The European Left and the Financial Crisis*, edited by M. Holmes & K. Roder. Manchester: Manchester University Press.

Raunio, T. 2010. "The EU and the welfare state are compatible: Finnish social democrats and European integration". *Government and Opposition* 45(2): 187–207.

Raunio, T. 2019. "Navigating through troubled times: the left and the euro crisis in Finland". In *The European Left and the Financial Crisis*, edited by M. Holmes & K. Roder. Manchester: Manchester University Press.

Recio, A. & J. Roca 2001. "The Spanish socialists in power: thirteen years of economic policy". In *Social Democracy in Neoliberal Times: The Left and Economic Policy since 1980*, edited by A. Glyn. Oxford: Oxford University Press.

Renner, K. 2017 [1930]. "A different Austria: into the decisive struggle". In *Austro-Marxism: The Ideology of Unity*, Vol. 2, *Changing the World: The Politics of Austro-Marxism*, edited by M. Blum & W. Smaldone. Leiden: Brill.

Rizzi, F. 1974. "From socialist unification to socialist scission 1969–69: socialist unification and the Italian party system". *Government and Opposition* 9(2): 146–64.

Roder, K. 2019. "In the shadow of Merkel: the German left and the crisis". In *The European Left and the Financial Crisis*, edited by M. Holmes & K. Roder. Manchester: Manchester University Press.

Rodrik, D. 2011. *The Globalization Paradox: Why Global Markets, States and Democracy Can't Coexist*. Oxford: Oxford University Press.

Rodrik, D. 2017. "The great globalization lie". *Prospect*, 12 December, https://www.prospectmagazine.co.uk/essays/45478/the-great-globalisation-lie.

Rodrik, D. 2022. "The new productivism paradigm". The Project Syndicate, 5 July, https://www.project-syndicate.org/commentary/new-productivism-economic-policy-paradigm-by-dani-rodrik-2022-07.

Rothstein, B. & S. Steinmo 2013. "Social democracy in crisis? What crisis?". In *The Crisis of Social Democracy in Europe*, edited by M. Keating & D. McCrone. Edinburgh: Edinburgh University Press.

Ryner, M. 2016. "Why the financial crisis has not generated a social democratic alternative in Europe?" In *European Social Democracy during the Global Economic Crisis: Renovation or Resignation?* edited by D. Bayley, J.-M. de Waele, F. Escalona & M. Vieira. Manchester: Manchester University Press.

Sandner, G. 2023. "From state party to party crisis: the Social Democratic Party of Austria". In *The Resistible Corrosion of Europe's Centre-Left after 2008*, edited by G. Menz. Abingdon: Routledge.

Santos, F. 1983. "Na Transição do 'Constitucionalismo Monárquico' Para o 'Constitucionalismo Republicano': A Crise do Partido Socialisre e a Crise do Partido Republicano". *Análise Social* 18(72–4): 673–85.

Sassoon, D. 1997. *One Hundred Years of Socialism: The West European Left in the Twentieth Century*. London: Fontana.

Sassoon, D. 2013. "The Long Depression, the Great Crash and socialism in western Europe". In *The Crisis of Social Democracy in Europe*, edited by M. Keating & D. McCrone. Edinburgh: Edinburgh University Press.

Scharpf, F. 1987. *Crisis and Choice in European Social Democracy*. Ithaca, NY: Cornell University Press.

Schmidt, I. 2016. "German social democracy: a popular project and an unpopular party", in *European Social Democracy during the Global Economic Crisis: Renovation or Resignation?*, edited by D. Bailey, J.-M. de Waele, F. Escalona and M. Vieira. Manchester: Manchester University Press.

Shaev, B. 2020. "Nationalism, transnationalism and European socialism: a comparison of the French and German cases". *History of European Ideas* 46(1): 41–58.

Shaw, B. 1961. *Essays in Fabian Socialism*. London: Constable.

Shaw, E. 2009. "New Labour and public sector reform". In *In Search of Social Democracy: Responses to Crisis and Modernisation*, edited by J. Callaghan, N. Fishman, B. Jackson & M. McIvor, 147–67. Manchester: Manchester University Press.

Shaw, E. 1994. *The Labour Party since 1979: Crisis and Transformation*. London: Routledge.

Slobodian, Q. 2018. *Globalists: The End of Empire and the Birth of Neoliberalism*. Cambridge, MA: Harvard University Press.

Smaldone, W. 2020. *European Socialism: A Concise History with Documents*, 2nd edition. London: Rowman & Littlefield.

Sotiropoulos, D. 2016. "Triumph and collapse: PASOK in the wake of the crisis in Greece, 2009–13". In *European Social Democracy during the Global Economic Crisis: Renovation or Resignation?*, edited by D. Bayley, J.-M. de Waele, F. Escalona & M. Vieira, 193–212. Manchester: Manchester University Press.

SPD 1959. *Godesberger Programm: Grundsatzprogramm der Sozialdemokratischen Partei Deutschlands*, 13–15 November. Berlin: Sozialdemokratische Partei Deutschland.

Stiglitz, J. 2013. *The Price of Inequality*. London: Penguin.

Streeck, W. 2014. *Buying Time: The Delayed Crisis of Democratic Capitalism*. London: Verso.

Streeck, W. & K. Thelen 2010. "Introduction: institutional change in advanced political economies". In *Beyond Continuity: Institutional Change in Advanced Political Economies*, edited by W. Streeck & K. Thelen. Oxford: Oxford University Press.

Sutcliffe-Braithwaite, F., A. Davies & B. Jackson 2021. "Introduction: a neoliberal age? Britain since the 1970s". In *The Neoliberal Age? Britain since the 1970s*, edited by A. Davies, B. Jackson & F. Sutcliffe-Braithwaite. London: UCL Press.

Taber, M. 2021. *Under the Socialist Banner: Resolutions of the Second International 1889–1912*. Chicago: Haymarket Books.

Tavits, M. & N. Letki 2009. "When left is right: party ideology and policy in post-communist Europe". *American Political Science Review* 103(4): 555–69.

Tilton, T. 1992. "The role of ideology in social democratic politics". In *Creating Social Democracy: A Century of the Social Democratic Labor Party in Sweden*, edited by K. Misgeld, K. Molin & K. Åmark, 409–27. University Park: Pennsylvania State University Press.

Tilton, T. 1979. "A Swedish road to socialism: Ernst Wigforss and the ideological foundations of Swedish social democracy". *American Political Science Review* 73(2): 505–20.

Tooze, A. 2018. *Crashed: How a Decade of Financial Crises Changed the World*. New York: Viking.

Tooze, A. 2022. "Welcome to the world of the polycrisis". *Financial Times*, 28 October, https://www.ft.com/content/498398e7-11b1-494b-9cd3-6d669dc3de33.

Touraine, A. 1983. *L'Après Socialisme*. Paris: Grasset.

Tsakalotos, E. 2001. "The political economy of social democratic economic policies: the PASOK experiment in Greece". In *Social Democracy in Neoliberal Times: The Left and Economic Policy since 1980*, edited by A. Glyn. Oxford: Oxford University Press.

Tsarouhas, D. 2009. "A new Swedish model? Swedish social democracy at the crossroads". In *In Search of Social Democracy*, edited by J. Callaghan, N. Fishman, B. Jackson & M. McIvor. Manchester: Manchester University Press.

Vachudova, M. 2013. "The positions and fortunes of social democratic parties in east central Europe". In *The Crisis of European Social Democracy*, edited by M. Keating & D. McCrone. Edinburgh: Edinburgh University Press.

Vandenbroucke, F. 2001. "European social democracy and the Third Way: convergence, divisions and shared questions". In *New Labour: The Progressive Future?*, edited by S. White. Basingstoke: Palgrave Macmillan.

Vartiainen, J. 2001. "Understanding Swedish social democracy: victims of success?" In *Social Democracy in Neoliberal Times: The Left and Economic Policy since 1980*, edited by A. Glyn. Oxford: Oxford University Press.

White, D. 1981. "Reconsidering European socialism in the 1920s". *Journal of Contemporary History* 16(2): 251–72.

Wickham-Jones, M. 2021. "Neoliberalism in the Labour Party". In *The Neoliberal Age? Britain since the 1970s*, edited by A. Davies, B. Jackson & F. Sutcliffe-Braithwaite, 226–53. London: UCL Press.

Wilkinson, R. & K. Pickett 2009. *The Spirit Level: Why More Equal Societies Almost Always Do Better*. London: Allen Lane.

World Bank 2022. *World Development Report 2022*, https://www.worldbank.org/en/publication/wdr2022.

Wright, T. 1997. *Why Vote Labour?* London: Penguin.

Wright, T. 1996. *Socialisms: Old and New*. London: Routledge.

Zariski, R. 1962. "The Italian Socialist Party: a case study in factional conflict". *American Political Science Review* 52(2): 373–90.

Zubek, V. 1994. "The reassertion of the left in post-communist Poland". *Europe-Asia Studies* 46(5): 801–37.

Index